I0199463

Proof of War

This is Joseph Bell McBride's story in pictures.

A family treasure finally shared.

Published by UmPrint Publishing 2018
umprint.net

Researched by Sherril Jennings

Contributions by Sherril Jennings

Narration available by Gwen Freeman

gallipolilanding.nz/ album-with-gwen

Photo reproductions, authoring and editing by Ryan L. Jennings

144p 1.2cm

ISBN Hardcover 978-0-473-43912-5
ISBN Softcover 978-0-473-43911-8

Inspired by New Zealanders

Original Gallipoli photo album photographs by Joseph Bell McBride / gallipolilanding.nz

A catalogue record for this book is available from the National Library of New Zealand.

Proof of War

Researched by

Sherril Jennings

Grand-daughter

Narrated by

Gwen Freeman

Daughter

Produced by

Ryan L. Jennings

Great-grandson

Table Of Contents

+

Regiment Number 12/1127

In Memory Of
Joseph McBride

The New Zealand Gallipoli Landing glass negative.

Photographed by Joseph McBride.

Joseph (Joe) Bell McBride captured the moment New Zealand soldiers landed at Gallipoli for the first time on April 25th 1915.

+

Joseph's photo album is reproduced here in its entirety for the first time, including the Gallipoli landing photograph that became a classic amongst archival records of significance. It reveals one New Zealand soldiers journey, of what took place before, during and after New Zealanders landed at Gallipoli on April 25th 1915.

The McBride Brothers

+

Joseph McBride and William McBride

Aged just 21 Joseph McBride was one of the four brothers in the family, who signed up for active duty and served in the Auckland Infantry Battalion. His brother William (Billy) didn't serve at Gallipoli, but they met later in Egypt.

Three brothers returned from the war. David, who was younger and joined later, was killed only a short time after arriving at the Etaples front, in France, in 1917.

Joseph and William gave him a five pound note for his 21st birthday. When he was killed, a few days later, he still had the money in his pocket. Tom enlisted after Gallipoli and embarked for Egypt.

David McBride

Tom McBride

The Medical Corps

+

Joe was a compassionate man, which led him to work in the medical corps.

Joseph McBride 2nd from left front row.

His work often placed him in the front line where he would have seen the sheer horror and brutality of what war does.

Joseph McBride shown in the middle. On return from Gallipoli, the horses were mostly shot, rather than bring them back or leave them to go hungry.

The Gallipoli Photo Album

+

The following photographs have been reproduced exactly in the same order as Joseph McBride set them out in the album over 100 years ago. It is the photographic journey of one soldier to places abroad, and what he recorded as events unfolded, that he believed would hold significance to New Zealanders.

It also shows what a young man believed worthy of capturing on film during his four years abroad at war. In amongst photos of troops gathering at the Great Sphinx of Giza and preparing for war, you'll find photos of curiosity including a giraffe, ostriches, a hippo, Turkish women wearing burkhas and children playing amongst soldiers.

The New Zealand Gallipoli Photo Album

Actual size 16cm x 12.5cm

MOHAMADDIN
INDIAN MASTER
TAILOR -

The El RIC ST

No I NZ Fd Amb

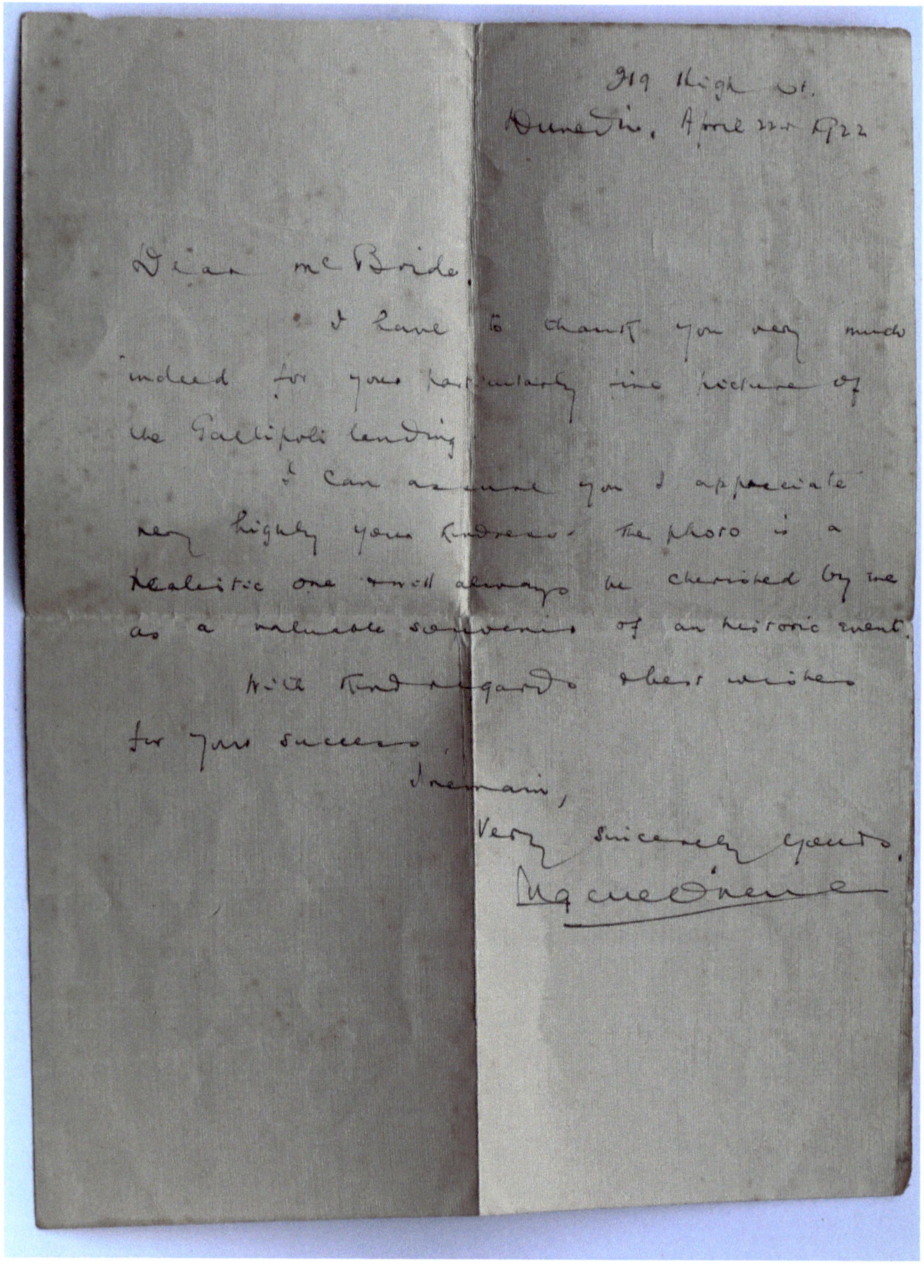

919 High St.
Dunedin, April 22nd 1922

Dear McBride,

I have to thank you very much indeed for your particularly fine picture of the Gallipoli landing.

I can assure you I appreciate very highly your kindness. The photo is a realistic one & will always be cherished by me as a valuable souvenir of an historic event.

With kind regards & best wishes for your success,

I remain,

Very sincerely yours,

[illegible]

219 High Street

Dunedin, April 22nd, 1922

Dear McBride,

I have to thank you very much indeed for your particularly fine picture of the Gallipoli landing.

I can assure you I appreciate very highly your kindness. The photo is a realistic one and will always be cherished by me as a valuable souvenir of an historic event.

With kind regards and best wishes for your success.

I remain,

very sincerely yours,

Eugene O'Neill

2/182 Major Eugene Joseph O'Neill and 3/273 Major Donald Norman Watson Murray, both of the New Zealand Medical Corps, posted to the 1st Field Ambulance sit at what appears to be the Dressing Station at the foot of Walker's Ridge on Ocean Beach, Gallipoli, 1915.

Photo 7/324 Captain William Deans
Acknowledgement: National Army Musuem of New Zealand

A Surgeon's Souvenir

+

Eugene O'Neill (Regiment No. 3/182) was the Attesting Officer on Joseph's enlistment and signed and witnessed his enlistment on 18th August 1914. Eugene enlisted two days later. Neither of them knew then that they would both be embarking for the Dardenelles eight months later on 12th April 1915.

Eugene was also enlisted in the New Zealand Medical Corps as a Surgeon serving with 1st field Ambulance and rising to Colonel. Joseph served his medical duties in No 4. NZ Field Ambulance and rose to Captain after the war.

Joseph McBride's original camera that took the photographs in the Gallipoli photo album.

Always A Photographer

+

Before the war, Joe was a keen photographer and may have used this camera in his work helping a professional photographer in Gore, Southland.

The camera is a Pocket Kodak with two dates inscribed on the front 'Mar 4th 1902' and 'May 6th 1913'.

The front of the Vest Pocket Kodak he took with him to photograph his journey.

The rear of the camera is well worn.

Getting Married

+

Violet Galt married Joseph and took the McBride name on 9th May 1923. He was 31. Violet and Joseph McBride were life-long companions until his death in 1970.

Joseph and Violet McBride.

The opening of the McBride Wing at Papanui High School.

First Principal
Of Papanui High School

+

Prior to the war, Joseph had been training for a teaching career at the time he signed up as a private and upon his return, he resumed that career.

On his return to New Zealand at the end of the war, he enrolled at Otago University and gained a BSc degree. He was appointed Principal of the new Papanui High School in 1936.

Portrait of Principal Joseph McBride being presented to the school.

His portrait hangs in the main block at Papanui High School and the framed photo in the McBride wing is named after him.

First principal of the school 1936 - 1952.

Giving Away The Bride

+

Violet and Joseph McBride with daughter Phyllis McBride (soon to be Dorreen) on her big day, before marrying William Dorreen.

Violet McBride, Phyllis McBride and Joseph McBride.

First Grandchild

+

Proud grandparents holding their first grandchild, Robyn Dorreen in their arms.

Robyn Dorreen, Violet McBride and Joseph McBride.

Family Life

+

He loved nothing more than to share his love of family at Christmas time. All of us grandchildren would be outside sitting on his neatly mown grass, peeling peas he had grown in his well tended vegetable garden.

From left to right: Bill Dorreen, Joseph McBride and Gwen Freeman.

Children: Robyn Dorreen, Sherril Dorreen, Meredith Dorreen,
David Verkerk, Stephen Freeman and Gwyneth Verkerk.

Joseph's Three Daughters

+

Phyllis Dorreen, Kathleen Verkerk and Gwen Freeman.

Gwen Freeman (Joseph's daughter) and Sherril Jennings (Joseph's grand-daughter) look through his photo album.

Read along with Gwen as she turns each photo album page at:

gallipolilanding.nz/album-with-gwen (25minute audio)

Gwen On The Gallipoli Photo Album

+

Dad never showed them to me. He gave me the photo of them landing at Gallipoli and he gave each of his daughters a photo of that and I shut it away. I didn't like looking at it.

This album gives you a picture of what it was like. I mean either you're walking or you're on a horse. I think Dad did a lot of work with soldiers coming out and getting injured. I never knew why he knew so much about what to do in an emergency but he was there. He never talked of his life over there. If Dad had done what he was told, we wouldn't be seeing these.

1. FRANSIZ ANITI VE MEZARLIĞI : Çanakkale Savaşları kayıpları için.

THE FRENCH MEMORIAL AND CEMETERY : To officers and men who fought in the Gallipoli Campaign.

2. HELLES ANITI : Çanakkale Savaşlarının kayıp Britanya Milletler Topluluğu askerleri için.

THE HELLES MEMORIAL : To Commonwealth officers and men who fell in the Gallipoli Campaign and have no known grave.

3. ÇANAKKALE ŞEHİTLER ABİDESİ : Çanakkale Savaşları (1915) kahramanları için.

THE TURKISH MEMORIAL : In honoured memory of the Turkish heroes who fell in the Gallipoli Campaign.

AIRMAIL - PAR AVION

23.10.72
Canakkale
Turkey.

Dear Gran,

Today we travelled from Istanbul to here passing Gallipoli on the way. We went and saw the memorials where all the Australians & New Zealanders are buried. From the top we could see the beach that I remember Grandad talking about so vividly. There seemed a strange silence from the top of the hill, almost as if all life had ceased. Not even birds in the trees. We then drove along the beach front and there are many more memorials along there. The huge expanse of land is covered with shrubs & pine trees. The tide was in and waves making the only movement in the blustery wind. I have taken several photos & movies. This postcard was the only one I could get but in actual fact shows the French Memorial & Helles Memorial. Hope you're well. Love Sherril

MRS. V. C. McBRIDE
15 TUDOR AVE,
ILAM
CHRISTCHURCH 4
NEW ZEALAND
(N.Z)

Postcard sent from Turkey from Sherril to her grandmother, Joseph's wife, Violet McBride, dated 23rd October 1972.

Sherril On the Gallipoli Photo Album

+

In 1974 while visiting my grandmother in Christchurch, she went to the polished sideboard and opened the top drawer to show me Grandad's photo album. She said she wanted me to have it as I had always been interested in photography and she knew I would look after it. It has always been a family treasure for me. My mother wanted the landing of Gallipoli photo attributed to her beloved Dad and I have continued with her wishes.

This is Joseph Bell McBrides story in pictures.

A family treasure finally shared.

Gwen Freeman viewing the reproduced Gallipoli Photo Album with Ryan Jennings.

Memories are passed down to the next generation but a photo album has its own memory.

This is what Gallipoli looked like.

These are the people.

This is the landscape.

This is the war.

These are the soldiers.

We will remember them.

New Zealand casualties in Gallipoli reference mch.govt.nz (D-0711278) April 2017 and Historian David Green ww100.govt.nz/how-many-new-zealanders-served-on-gallipoli-some-new-answers

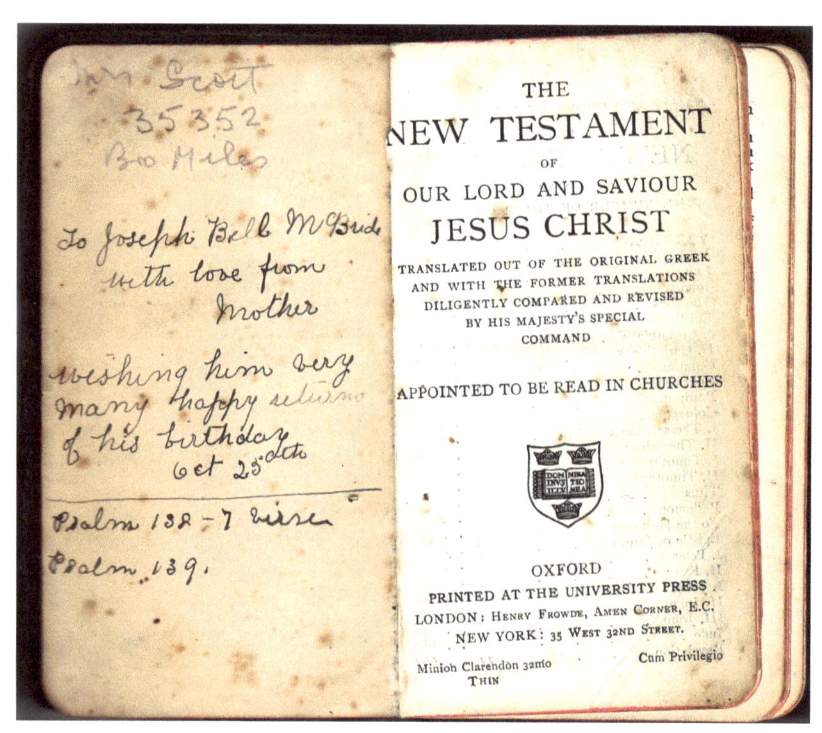
To Joseph Bell McBride
with love from
Mother

wishing him very
many happy returns
of his birthday
Oct 25th

Psalm 138 - 7 verse

Psalm 139.

THE
NEW TESTAMENT
OF
OUR LORD AND SAVIOUR
JESUS CHRIST
TRANSLATED OUT OF THE ORIGINAL GREEK
AND WITH THE FORMER TRANSLATIONS
DILIGENTLY COMPARED AND REVISED
BY HIS MAJESTY'S SPECIAL
COMMAND

APPOINTED TO BE READ IN CHURCHES

OXFORD
PRINTED AT THE UNIVERSITY PRESS
LONDON: HENRY FROWDE, AMEN CORNER, E.C.
NEW YORK: 35 WEST 32ND STREET.

Minion Clarendon 32mo
THIN

Cum Privilegio

The bible gifted to Joseph by his mother
for his birthday on October 25th.

Joe was given the ANZAC Commemorative Medallion in 1967. Contained within a plush purple velvet box. Along with it, there was a lapel badge sized version given to him which we was to be worn on ANZAC Day.

The rear of the ANZAC medal is inscribed with "J B Mc Bride". This bronze medallion was instituted in 1967 and awarded to Australian and New Zealand personnel who participated in the Gallipoli campaign in 1915.

Discover More

+

While these photos provide a level of clarity on what Joseph McBride experienced, it also creates unanswered questions. By sharing this family treasure, we hope that distinguished researchers, archivists, Gallipoli historians and descendants of the Main Body of the New Zealand Expeditionary Force may be able to cross-reference their knowledge with Joseph's Gallipoli photo album to enrich this record of New Zealands history.

Make a submission at:

gallipolilanding.nz/proof-of-war

Successful submissions will be included in the next edition with attribution.

A Foundation For The Future

+

All proceeds from this book go towards helping the next generation fulfill their potential to the highest possible level.

Papanui High School Alumni Newsletter

Volume 6 Issue 2

2 June 2012

Joseph Bell McBride (Scotty) Principal 1936-52

Mr McBride's granddaughter and great grandson called into the school recently to view the Anzac photo which he is famous for and also the Bill Moore (now a well known artist) portrait taken when Mr McBride was Principal and Bill a student here. This portrait has 'pride of place' in the main stairway to the staff room.

We were glad to hear that Mr McBride's recent great great grandson has also been named **Joseph**.

Joseph McBride as a young man.

Joseph's Military Personnel Files

+

Joseph's Military Personnel Files reveal where he travelled while taking the photographs during the 1,626 days he served overseas. For the first time, it connects the photos he took with the locations he was stationed.

Gallipoli Landing	Dardenelles	Cairo Egypt	Ghezirah Egypt	Ismailia Egypt	Almeria France
25th Apr 1915	12th Dec 1915	15th Dec 1915	31st Dec 1915	18th Jan 1916	6th Apr 1916

Born	Enlisted	Embarked	Discharged	Married
25th Oct 1892	18th Aug 1914	12th Apr 1915	11th Apr 1919	9th May 1923

Promoted To Corporal — 13th Oct 1915

England — 1st Apr 1917

France — 20th May 1917

England — 14th Nov 1917

Codford England — 11th May 1918

Embarked Melbourne — 25th Jan 1919

Promoted to Captain — 20th Apr 1926

Papanui High School Principal — 1936 – 1952

Commemorative Medallion — 1967

Died — 1970

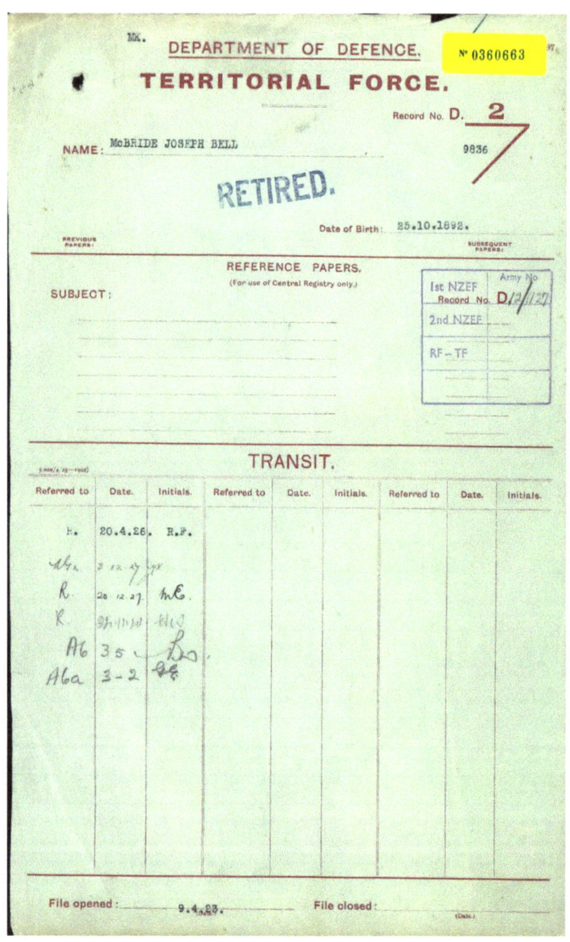

MK.

DEPARTMENT OF DEFENCE.

Nº 0360663

TERRITORIAL FORCE.

Record No. D. 2/9836

NAME: McBRIDE JOSEPH BELL

RETIRED.

Date of Birth: 25.10.1892.

REFERENCE PAPERS.
(For use of Central Registry only.)

SUBJECT:

1st NZEF Record No. D/12/127
2nd NZEF
RF – TF

TRANSIT.

Referred to	Date.	Initials.	Referred to	Date.	Initials.	Referred to	Date.	Initials.
R.	20.4.26.	R.F.						
[illegible]	3.12.27	[illegible]						
R.	20.12.27	mE.						
R.	[illegible]	[illegible]						
A6	3 5	[illegible]						
A6a	3-2	[illegible]						

File opened: 9.4.23. File closed:

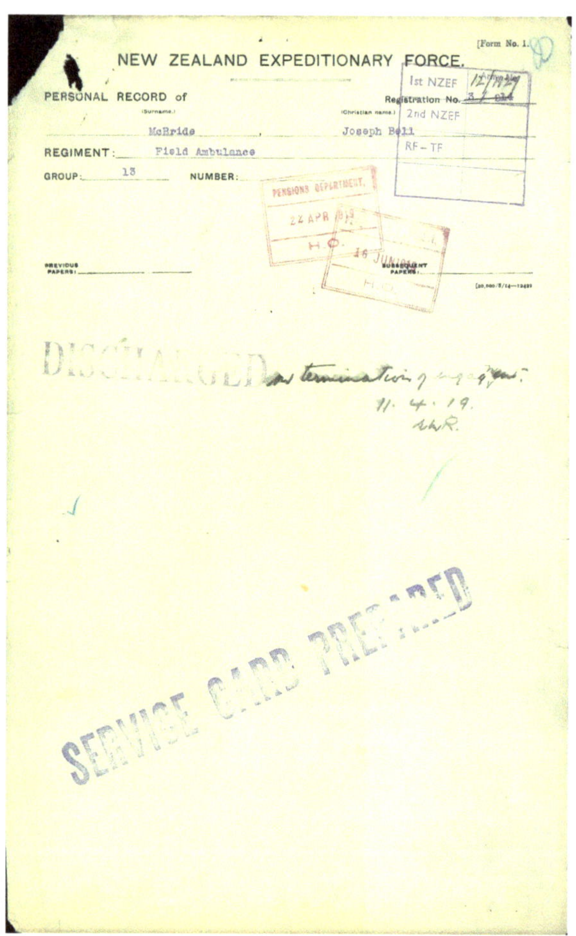

[Form No. 1.]

NEW ZEALAND EXPEDITIONARY FORCE.

PERSONAL RECORD of McBride Joseph Bell

1st NZEF Registration No. 12/1927
2nd NZEF
RF – TF

REGIMENT: Field Ambulance

GROUP: 13 NUMBER:

PENSIONS DEPARTMENT. 22 APR 1919 H.O.

DISCHARGED on termination of engagement. 11.4.19.

SERVICE CARD PREPARED

This form to be used for Officers of the N.Z. Territorial Force, and is to be kept immediately under cover of Personal File.

[Army Form N.Z. (B) T.

9836

NEW ZEALAND TERRITORIAL FORCE.

ATTESTATION FOR GENERAL SERVICE IN NEW ZEALAND

of Joseph Bell McBride

in the 4th (Cadet) B. Canterbury Regiment.

(Questions to be answered by Candidate.)

1. What is your full name?	1. Joseph Bell McBride
2. In what country and upon what date were you born?	2. New Zealand: 25th Oct, 1892
3. If of alien birth state when and where you were naturalized	3. -
4. If born overseas state the period of your residence in New Zealand	4. -
5. In what countries were your parents born?	5. Ireland (Father) New Zealand (Mother)
6. If your parents were of alien birth state when and where they were naturalized	6. —— (Father) (Mother)
7. Are your married?	7. Yes.
8. If so, in what country was your wife born?	8. New Zealand.
9. Who is your next-of-kin (State relationship)?	9. Mr R. McBride (father)
10. What is that person's postal address?	10. Charlton P.O.; Via Gore, Southland
11. What are your educational qualifications?	11. B. Sc
12. What is your trade or calling?	12. School Teacher.
13. By whom were you last employed?	13. Student, Otago University
14. Have you ever been sentenced to imprisonment by the Civil or military power?	14. No.
15. Give the details of any previous service in the British Naval or Military Forces, and enumerate any decorations or medals you hold	15. 4 6/12 months N.Z. Expeditionary Force 1914-15 Star, Brit. Victory, Gen. Service medals
16. Have you ever been rejected as unfit for military service? If so, give details	16. No.
17. Are you willing to be vaccinated or inoculated as may be required by competent authority?	17. Yes
18. Are you willing to serve in any Unit of the New Zealand Territorial Force in New Zealand until lawfully struck off strength or discharged?	18. Yes
19. Are you willing to serve under the Regulations for the New Zealand Military Forces and be subject to the Imperial Army Act until struck off strength or discharged?	19. Yes

DEFENCE D. 1[illegible] APR 1923 CHRISTCHURCH

I, Joseph Bell McBride, do solemnly declare that the above answers made by me to the above questions are true, and that I am willing to fulfil the engagement made.

Signature of Candidate: Joseph B McBride

Signature of Witness: [illegible signature]

Oath to be taken by candidate on attestation.

I, Joseph Bell McBride, do sincerely promise and swear that I will be faithful and bear true allegiance to His Majesty King George the Fifth, his heirs and successors, and that I will faithfully serve in the New Zealand Territorial Force until I shall be lawfully struck off strength or discharged.

Certificate of Attesting Officer.

The above questions were read to the above-named candidate in my presence. I have taken care that he understands each question, and that his answer to each question has been duly entered as replied to, and the said candidate has made and signed the declaration and taken the oath before me, at Christchurch, on this 9 day of April, 1923

Signature of Attesting Officer: [illegible signature]

Commission issued on

If any alteration is required on this page of the Attestation, the Attesting Officer should be requested to make it and initial the alteration.

(D. 44/533.)

(6,000/8/21—11/33

3

PROMOTIONS, CASUALTIES, TRANSFERS, ETC.

Rank.	Date.	Unit.	—	—

DETAILS OF WAR SERVICE.

4 6/12 years non-commissioned in Medical Corps NZEF

DECORATIONS AND MEDALS AWARDED.

1914/15 Star, Victory, & G S medals

4

EXAMINATIONS FOR PROMOTIONS PASSED.

Nature of Examination.	Date passed.	Percentage of Marks obtained.	Remarks.	Initials.

SPECIAL COURSES OF INSTRUCTION PASSED.

Nature of Course.	Locality.	Qualifications obtained.	Remarks.	Initials.

Details of past service in the New Zealand Military Forces, showing whether efficient or otherwise by "training years": [illegible]

Certified a correct record. [illegible], Capt. N.Z.S.C.

Details of subsequent service in the New Zealand Military Forces, showing whether efficient or otherwise by "training years":

Certified a correct record.

Date posted to reserve, or retired list, or struck off strength:

Entries on this page must be certified correct by an Officer of the New Zealand Permanent Forces.

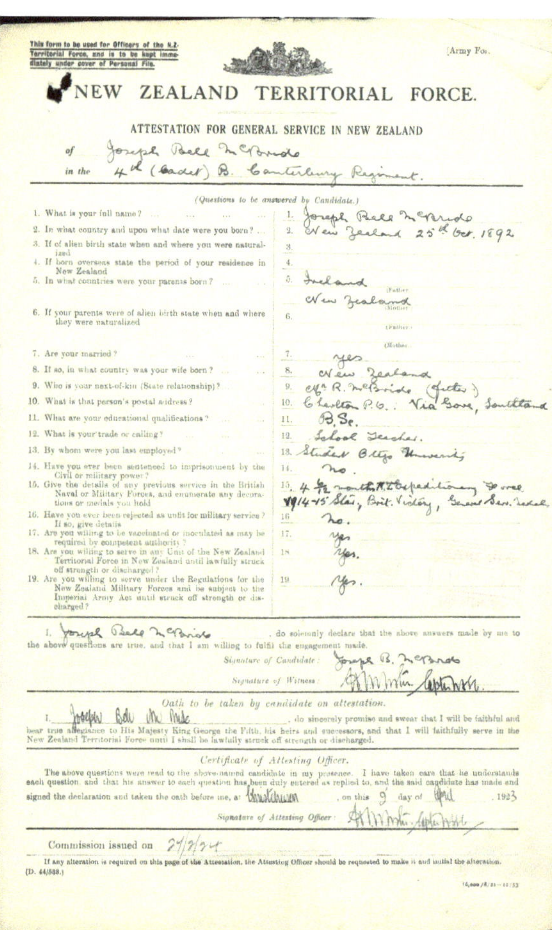

This form to be used for Officers of the N.Z. Territorial Force, and is to be kept immediately under cover of Personal File.

(Army Fo.

NEW ZEALAND TERRITORIAL FORCE.

ATTESTATION FOR GENERAL SERVICE IN NEW ZEALAND

of Joseph Bell McBride

in the 4th (Cadet) B. Canterbury Regiment.

(Questions to be answered by Candidate.)

1. What is your full name?	1. Joseph Bell McBride
2. In what country and upon what date were you born?	2. New Zealand 25th Oct. 1892
3. If of alien birth state when and where you were naturalized	3.
4. If born overseas state the period of your residence in New Zealand	4.
5. In what countries were your parents born?	5. Ireland (Father) New Zealand (Mother)
6. If your parents were of alien birth state when and where they were naturalized	6. (Father) (Mother)
7. Are your married?	7. Yes
8. If so, in what country was your wife born?	8. New Zealand
9. Who is your next-of-kin (State relationship)?	9. Mr R. McBride (father)
10. What is that person's postal address?	10. Charlton P.O.: Via Gore, Southland
11. What are your educational qualifications?	11. B.Sc.
12. What is your trade or calling?	12. School Teacher.
13. By whom were you last employed?	13. Student Otago University
14. Have you ever been sentenced to imprisonment by the Civil or military power?	14. No.
15. Give the details of any previous service in the British Naval or Military Forces, and enumerate any decorations or medals you hold	15. 4 1/2 months N.Z. Expeditionary Force. 1914-15 Star, Brit. Victory, General Serv. Medal.
16. Have you ever been rejected as unfit for military service? If so, give details	16. No.
17. Are you willing to be vaccinated or inoculated as may be required by competent authority?	17. Yes
18. Are you willing to serve in any Unit of the New Zealand Territorial Force in New Zealand until lawfully struck off strength or discharged?	18. Yes.
19. Are you willing to serve under the Regulations for the New Zealand Military Forces and be subject to the Imperial Army Act until struck off strength or discharged?	19. Yes.

I, Joseph Bell McBride, do solemnly declare that the above answers made by me to the above questions are true, and that I am willing to fulfil the engagement made.

Signature of Candidate: Joseph B. McBride

Signature of Witness: [illegible] Capt. N.Z.S.C.

Oath to be taken by candidate on attestation.

I, Joseph Bell McBride, do sincerely promise and swear that I will be faithful and bear true allegiance to His Majesty King George the Fifth, his heirs and successors, and that I will faithfully serve in the New Zealand Territorial Force until I shall be lawfully struck off strength or discharged.

Certificate of Attesting Officer.

The above questions were read to the above-named candidate in my presence. I have taken care that he understands each question, and that his answer to each question has been duly entered as replied to, and the said candidate has made and signed the declaration and taken the oath before me, at Christchurch, on this 9 day of April, 1923

Signature of Attesting Officer: [illegible] Capt. N.Z.S.C.

Commission issued on 27/2/24

If any alteration is required on this page of the Attestation, the Attesting Officer should be requested to make it and initial the alteration.

(D. 44/588.)

16,000/8/21—11/53

2

Personal Description.

Apparent age: ________ years ________ months.
(To be determined according to the instructions given in the Regulations for Army Medical Service.)

Height: ________ feet ________ inches.

Weight: ________ lb.

Chest-measurement: Minimum, ________ inches.
Maximum, ________ inches.

Complexion:

Colour of eyes:

Colour of hair:

Religious profession:

Distinctive marks, and marks indicating congenital peculiarities or previous disease.

Medical Examination.

(Questions to be addressed to the Candidate by the Examining Officer.)

1. Have you ever had a fit? ... ... 1.
2. Have you ever had any other illnesses. If so, of what nature where these? 2.

I declare my answers to the above questions to be true and complete.

Signature of Candidate:

Date:

Details of Medical Examination.

Sight: Right eye,
,, Left eye,
Hearing: Right ear,
,, Left ear,
Colour-vision:
Are his limbs well formed?
Are the movements of all his joints full and perfect?
Is his chest well formed?
Is his heart normal?
Are his lungs normal?
What is the condition of the teeth?

Is he free from hernia?
Is he free from varicocele?
Is he free from varicose veins?
Is he free from hæmorrhoids?
Is he free from inveterate or contagious skin-disease?
Is there a distinct mark of vaccination?
Is he in good bodily and mental health and free from any physical defect likely to interfere with the efficient performance of his duties?
Are there any slight defects, but not sufficient to cause rejection?

Remarks.

Certificate of Medical Examination.

I HAVE examined this candidate and find that he does not present / presents any of the causes of rejection specified in the Regulations for Army Medical Services.

I consider him fit / unfit for active service.

________, 192 ________, Medical Officer.

Address:

3

PROMOTIONS, CASUALTIES, TRANSFERS, ETC.

Rank.	Date.	Unit.	—	—
2/Lt (P)	19/4/23	3rd(C)Bn. C.R.	Gaz 47/23	
2/Lt.	17/11/23	" "	G.O. 29/24	
Lieut	1/12/24	" "	Gaz 85/26	
Capt.	1/12/27	" "	G. 86/27	
"	1/9/31	4(C) Bn. C.R.	G.O. 287/31	
"	26.4.45.	"	R of O Class IIb.	S/Hs 137/45
Captain	5.2.48	Cant. Regt.	Retired List.	[illegible]

DETAILS OF WAR SERVICE.

4½ years non-Commissioned in Medical Corps NZEF

DECORATIONS AND MEDALS AWARDED.

1914/15 Star Victory & [illegible]

4

EXAMINATIONS FOR PROMOTIONS PASSED.

Nature of Examination.	Date passed.	Percentage of Marks obtained.	Remarks.	Initials.
Examination A	12/4/23		G.O. 99/23	
B	17/2/26		190/26	

SPECIAL COURSES OF INSTRUCTION PASSED.

Nature of Course.	Locality.	Qualifications obtained.	Remarks.	Initials.

Details of past service in the New Zealand Military Forces, showing whether efficient or otherwise by "training years": NIL

Certified a correct record. [signature]

Details of subsequent service in the New Zealand Military Forces, showing whether efficient or otherwise by "training years":

Certified a correct record.

Date posted to reserve, or retired list, or struck off strength:

Entries on this page must be certified correct by an Officer of the New Zealand Permanent Forces.

[Extract from *New Zealand Gazette* No. 8, 12th February, 1948, page 161]

Appointment, Relinquishment of Commission, and Retirements of Officers of the New Zealand Military Forces

Army Department,
Wellington, 11th February, 1948.

HIS Excellency the Governor-General has been pleased to approve of the following appointment, relinquishment of commission, and retirements of officers of the New Zealand Military Forces:—

REGULAR FORCE

N.Z. REGIMENT

The notice published in the *New Zealand Gazette* No. 50, dated 18th July, 1946, relative to Major (*temp.* Lieutenant-Colonel) G. M. McCaskill (then N.Z. Staff Corps) relinquishing the temporary rank of Lieutenant-Colonel, is hereby cancelled.

THE ROYAL N.Z. ELECTRICAL AND MECHANICAL ENGINEERS

6352 Sergeant Arthur Claude Weddell is granted the honorary rank of Lieutenant and Quartermaster for the duration of the Regular Force Officer Candidates' Course No. 5. Dated 29th January, 1948.

N.Z. TEMPORARY STAFF

Temp. Captain S. L. Wood is posted to the Retired List with the rank of Captain. Dated 6th February, 1948.

RESERVE OF OFFICERS

The undermentioned officers are posted to the Retired List:—

Major S. W. Turley.
Major A. R. Ryder.
Captain and Quartermaster G. J. Morrall.
Captain and Quartermaster H. S. Bannister.
Hon. Lieutenant G. M. Kirton.
Hon. Lieutenant S. Martin.
Hon. Lieutenant A. Dobson.
2nd Lieutenant W. H. Yorke, M.C., with the rank of Lieutenant.

Dated 28th January, 1948.

Lieutenant-Colonel E. M. Mackersey, E.D.
Major W. Fraser, V.D.
Major H. D. Tait.
Major J. A. McQueen, E.D.
Major and Quartermaster T. J. L. Buxton, V.D.
Captain N. R. W. Thomas.
Captain W. F. C. Balham, V.D.
Captain R. H. Nimmo, V.D.
Captain F. G. Yeo.
Captain J. A. Duffy, V.D.
Captain S. Frickleton, V.C.
Captain J. W. Bright.
Captain H. R. Biss, with the rank of Major.
Lieutenant J. T. Hill, V.D.
Lieutenant C. G. Dunham.
Lieutenant H. F. Brock.
Lieutenant J. P. C. Walshe.
Lieutenant G. S. Coldham, with the rank of Captain.
Lieutenant R. V. A. Knox.
2nd Lieutenant G. F. Penlington, with the rank of Captain.

Dated 29th January, 1948.

Major S. Marshall, D.C.M.
Major E. S. Harston.
Major and Quartermaster F. N. Whitcombe.
Captain A. C. Rowe.
Hon. Lieutenant C. W. McConnell.
Hon. Lieutenant H. C. A. Fox.
Sister G. M. T. Piggot.

Dated 2nd February, 1948.

Major-General Sir William L. H. Sinclair-Burgess, K.B.E., C.B., C.M.G., D.S.O.
Major-General Sir John E. Duigan, K.B.E., C.B., D.S.O.
Colonel Sir Stephen S. Allen, K.B.E., C.M.G., D.S.O., V.D.
Colonel F. Symon, C.B., C.M.G., D.S.O.
Hon. Colonel N. P. Adams, C.M.G.
Lieutenant-Colonel W. S. McCrorie, V.D.
Lieutenant-Colonel D. A. C. Lilburne, E.D.
Major H. M. Clark, V.D.
Major A. G. B. Price.
Major J. J. Keen, E.D.
Major D. G. Smith.
Major G. Cawte, V.D.
Major G. Mathias, M.C.
Major W. Smith.
Captain (*temp.* Major) F. S. Mintrom, M.C., M.M., with the rank of Major.
Major J. W. Crampton.
Captain W. Fergie.
Captain A. A. E. Pennefather.
Captain J. D. McArthur.
Captain J. B. McBride.
Captain S. E. Gilshnan, M.M., E.D., with the rank of Major.
Captain L. J. B. Chapple, E.D.
Captain B. A. Y. Wynne-Yorke.
Lieutenant (*temp.* Major) J. M. Russell, with the rank of Major.
Lieutenant A. J. Breach.
Lieutenant E. M. Gibbs.
Hon. Lieutenant E. Tregilgas.

Dated 3rd February, 1948.

The Wellington Regiment (City of Wellington's Own)

Lieutenant C. Meachen is posted to the Retired List with the honorary rank of Major. Dated 26th February, 1946.

SUPPLEMENTARY LIST

Captain H. C. Stead relinquishes his commission. Dated 13th November, 1947.

OFFICER STRUCK OFF THE STRENGTH OF THE 2ND NEW ZEALAND EXPEDITIONARY FORCE

Colonel (*temp.* Brigadier) R. H. Quilliam, C.B.E., and is posted to the Retired List with the rank of Brigadier. Dated 31st January, 1948.

F. JONES, Minister of Defence.

E. V. PAUL, Government Printer, Wellington.

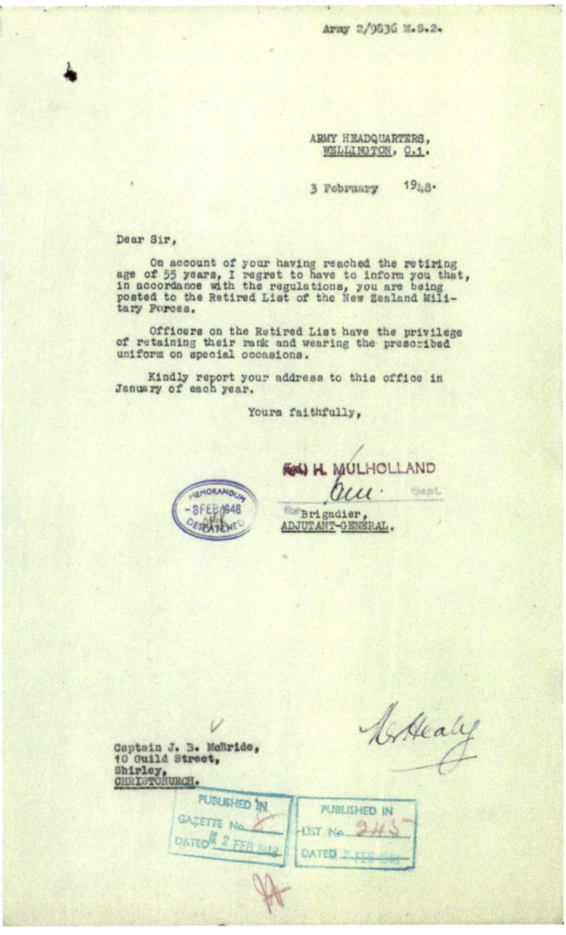

Army 2/9836 M.S.2.

ARMY HEADQUARTERS,
WELLINGTON, C.1.

3 February 1948.

Dear Sir,

On account of your having reached the retiring age of 55 years, I regret to have to inform you that, in accordance with the regulations, you are being posted to the Retired List of the New Zealand Military Forces.

Officers on the Retired List have the privilege of retaining their rank and wearing the prescribed uniform on special occasions.

Kindly report your address to this office in January of each year.

Yours faithfully,

(Sgd) H. MULHOLLAND
Capt.
Brigadier,
ADJUTANT-GENERAL.

MEMORANDUM -3 FEB 1948 DESPATCHED

Captain J. B. McBride,
10 Guild Street,
Shirley,
CHRISTCHURCH.

PUBLISHED IN GAZETTE No. 8 DATED 12 FEB 1948

PUBLISHED IN LIST No. 2435 DATED 2 FEB 1948

NEW ZEALAND MILITARY FORCES.

RESIGNATION, TRANSFER TO THE RESERVE OF OFFICERS, OR RETIREMENT OF AN OFFICER OF TERRITORIAL FORCE.

UNIT: PAPANUI TECHNICAL COLLEGE CADETS

Name. (Surname in block letters, to be followed by Christian names in full.)	Present Rank.	Highest Rank held in New Zealand Expeditionary Force.	Date of Birth.	Length of Commissioned Service in New Zealand Forces.	Address.
McBRIDE, JOSEPH BELL	CAPTAIN	Sgt.	25/10/1892	21 yrs	10 Guild Street, Shirley, CHRISTCHURCH.

1. *To the Officer Commanding* Area 10.

I, the above-named officer, hereby tender my application to

~~(1) Resign my commission. (This means severing all connection with the Military Forces.)~~

(2) Be transferred to the RESERVE OF OFFICERS {Class I (b). Class II (b).

(To be eligible for posting to the Reserve of Officers, an officer must—(a) have been on active service as a commissioned officer; or (b) have served as an officer in the New Zealand Permanent Forces; or (c) have served as an officer in the Territorial Force for four years.

~~(3) Be posted to the RETIRED LIST.~~

(To be eligible for posting to the Retired List an officer must—(a) have been on active service as a commissioned officer; or (b) have served as a commissioned officer for not less than ten years (towards which period service on the Reserve of Officers counts half-time); or (c) have served as an officer of the New Zealand Permanent Forces for not less than four years.)

Signature of officer Jos. B. McBride *Date* 26th April 1945

To the Staff Officer
i/c No. Regimental District.
Forwarded and recommended.
Commanding.
(Note.—The Adjutant will inform the Brigade Commander.)

3. *Headquarters,*
Southern Military District
Forwarded and recommended.
R Hitmonth Major
Staff Officer i/c No. 10 Regimental District.
Date 30 Apr 45

4. *General Headquarters,*
Wellington.
Forwarded and recommended.
Brigadier
District Commandant
Southern Military District
Commanding.
Date 1 MAY 1945

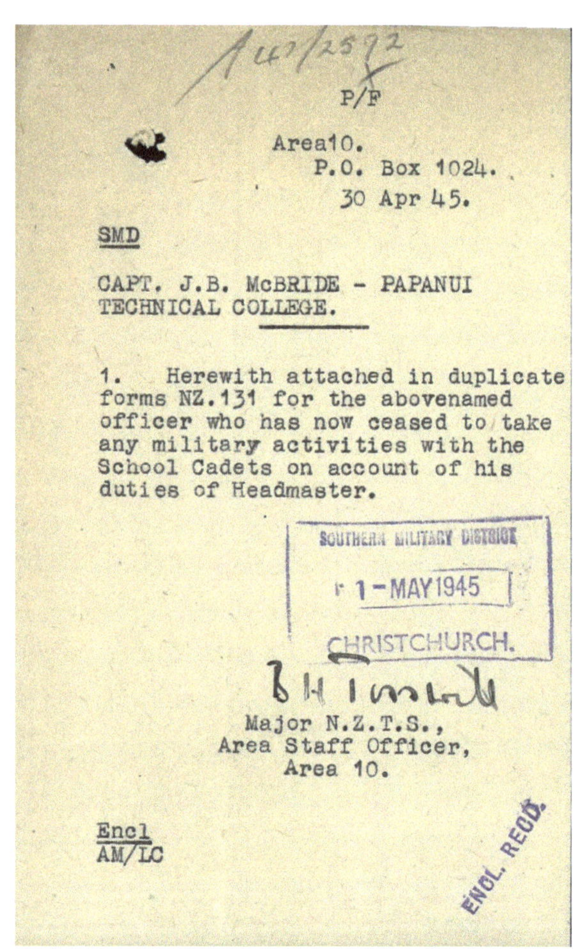
A41/2592

P/F

Area 10.
P.O. Box 1024.
30 Apr 45.

SMD

CAPT. J.B. McBRIDE - PAPANUI TECHNICAL COLLEGE.

1. Herewith attached in duplicate forms NZ.131 for the abovenamed officer who has now ceased to take any military activities with the School Cadets on account of his duties of Headmaster.

SOUTHERN MILITARY DISTRICT
1 - MAY 1945
CHRISTCHURCH.

Major N.Z.T.S.,
Area Staff Officer,
Area 10.

Encl
AM/LC

ENCL. RECD.

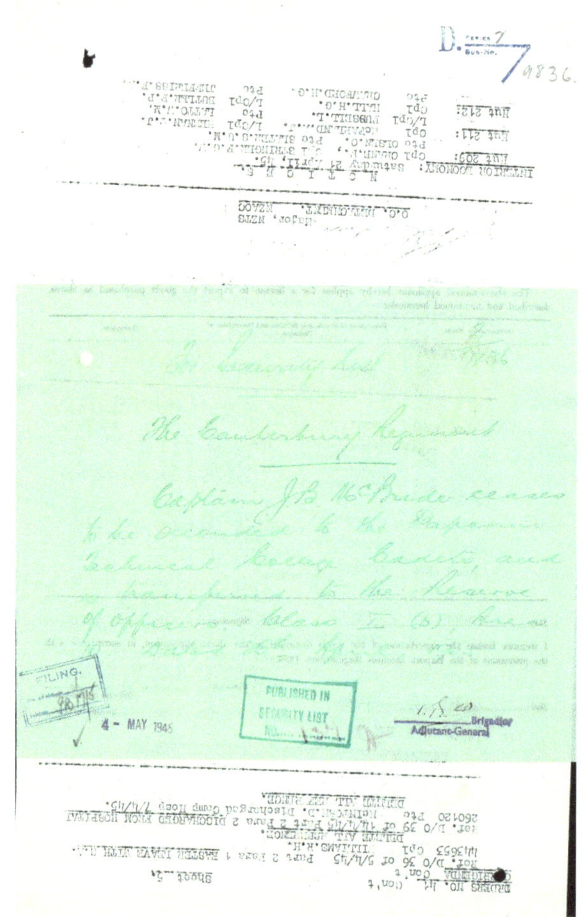
For Security List

The Canterbury Regiment

Captain J.B McBride ceases to be seconded to the Papanui Technical College Cadets, and is transferred to the Reserve of Officers, Class I (b) Area 10.

PUBLISHED IN SECURITY LIST

4 - MAY 1945

Brigadier
Adjutant-General

For Security List
The Canterbury Regiment

Captain J.B McBride ceases to be seconded to the Papanui Technical College Cadets, and is transferred to the Reserve of Officers, Class I (b) Area 10.

Dated 26th April, 1945.

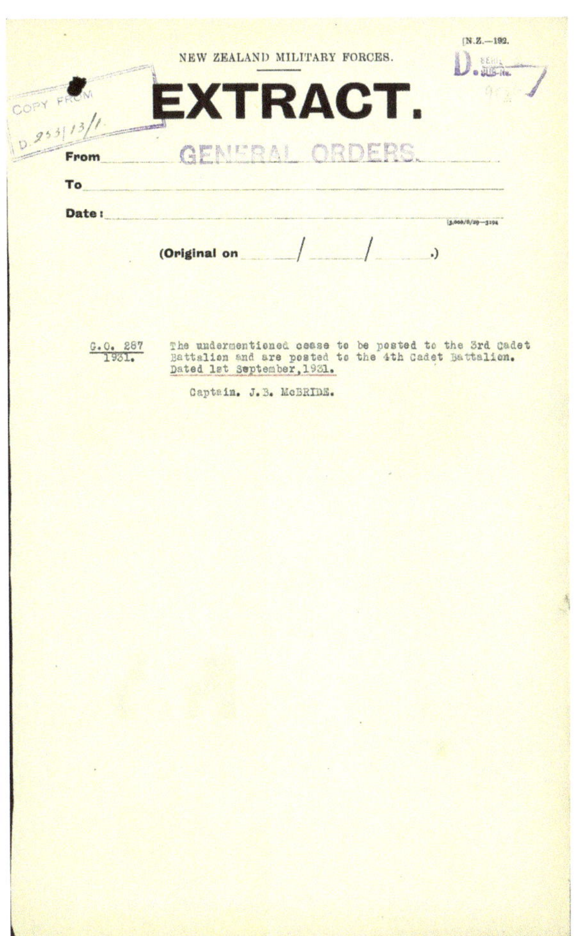

[N.Z.—192.

NEW ZEALAND MILITARY FORCES.

D. 9836/7

COPY FROM D. 233/13/1

EXTRACT.

From GENERAL ORDERS.

To

Date:

(Original on / / .)

G.O. 287 1931.   The undermentioned cease to be posted to the 3rd Cadet Battalion and are posted to the 4th Cadet Battalion. Dated 1st September, 1931.

Captain. J.B. McBRIDE.

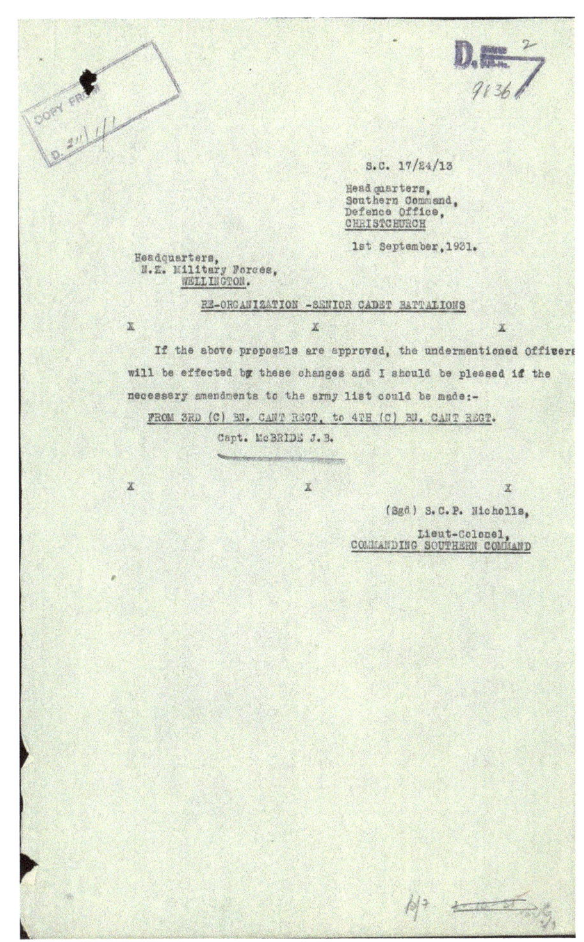

D. 9836/7

COPY FROM D. 211/1/1

S.C. 17/24/13

Headquarters,
Southern Command,
Defence Office,
CHRISTCHURCH

1st September, 1931.

Headquarters,
N.Z. Military Forces,
WELLINGTON.

RE-ORGANIZATION -SENIOR CADET BATTALIONS

X X X

If the above proposals are approved, the undermentioned Officers will be effected by these changes and I should be pleased if the necessary amendments to the army list could be made:-

FROM 3RD (C) BN. CANT REGT. to 4TH (C) BN. CANT REGT.

Capt. McBRIDE J.B.

X X X

(Sgd) S.C.P. Nicholls,

Lieut-Colonel,
COMMANDING SOUTHERN COMMAND

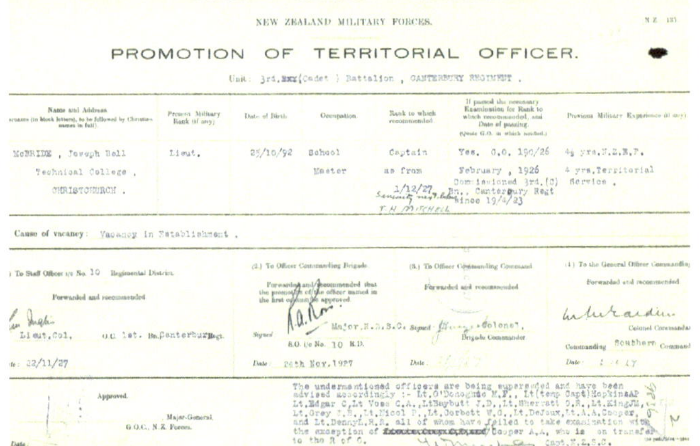

NEW ZEALAND MILITARY FORCES. N.Z. 131

PROMOTION OF TERRITORIAL OFFICER.

Unit: 3rd. (Cadet) Battalion, CANTERBURY REGIMENT.

Name and Address (surname (in block letters), to be followed by Christian names in full)	Present Military Rank (if any)	Date of Birth	Occupation	Rank to which recommended	If passed the necessary Examination for Rank to which recommended, and Date of passing (Quote G.O. in which notified.)	Previous Military Experience (if any)
McBRIDE, Joseph Bell Technical College, CHRISTCHURCH.	Lieut.	25/10/92	School Master	Captain as from 1/12/27 Seniority next below T.H. MITCHELL	Yes. G.O. 190/26 February, 1926 Commissioned 3rd.(C) Bn., Canterbury Regt since 19/4/23	4½ yrs. N.Z.E.F. 4 yrs. Territorial Service.

Cause of vacancy: Vacancy in Establishment.

(1.) To Staff Officer i/c No. 10 Regimental District. Forwarded and recommended. Lieut. Col. O.C. 1st. Bn. Canterbury Regt. Date: 22/11/27

(2.) To Officer Commanding Brigade. Forwarded and recommended that the promotion of the officer named in the first column be approved. Signed Major, N.Z.S.C. S.O. i/c No. 10 R.D. Date: 24th Nov. 1927

(3.) To Officer Commanding Command. Forwarded and recommended. Signed Colonel, Brigade Commander. Date:

(4.) To the General Officer Commanding. Forwarded and recommended. Colonel Commandant Commanding Southern Command. Date:

Approved. Major-General G.O.C. N.Z. Forces. Date:

The undermentioned officers are being superseded and have been advised accordingly :- Lt. O'Donoghue M.F., Lt(temp Capt) Hopkins A.P. Lt. Edgar C, Lt Voss C.A., Lt Baybutt J.D., Lt. Sherratt G.R., Lt. King J.M., Lt. Grey J.E., Lt. Nicol P., Lt. Corbett W.G., Lt. DeJoux, Lt. A.A. Cooper, and Lt. Denny L.R.R. all of whom have failed to take examination with the exception of Cooper A.A. who is on transfer to the R of O.

Capt. N.Z.S.C. Adjutant, 1st Bn, Canty. Regt

[Extract from *New Zealand Gazette* No. 86, 15th December, 1927.]

Page 3695.

Appointments, Promotions, Resignations, and Transfers of Officers of the N.Z. Military Forces.

Department of Defence,
Wellington, 12th December, 1927.

HIS Excellency the Governor-General has been pleased to approve of the appointments, promotions, resignations, and transfers of the undermentioned officers of the New Zealand Military Forces.

THE AUCKLAND MOUNTED RIFLES.

The appointment of 2nd Lieutenant (*on probation*) L. M. Nutt lapses. Dated 29th November, 1927.

THE NORTH AUCKLAND MOUNTED RIFLES.

John Lionel Rayner to be 2nd Lieutenant. Dated 30th November, 1927.

THE NELSON, MARLBOROUGH MOUNTED RIFLES.

Lieutenant F. H. P. Rogers to be Captain. Dated 17th September, 1927.

CORPS OF N.Z. ENGINEERS.

Northern Depot.

The appointment of 2nd Lieutenant (*on probation*) K. W. Fortune lapses. Dated 29th November, 1927.

THE N.Z. INFANTRY.

The Auckland Regiment (Countess of Ranfurly's Own.)

The appointments of the undermentioned 2nd Lieutenants (*on probation*) lapse. Dated 29th November, 1927.

E. D. Pritchard, 1st Battalion.
T. Scott, 1st Battalion.
J. S. Clapham, 1st Battalion.
J. K. Asher, 1st Battalion.
W. La Roche, 2nd C Battalion.
W. G. V. Fernie, 2nd C Battalion.
W. A. Macky, 2nd C Battalion.
C. N. Nicholls, 2nd C Battalion.
E. M. Blaiklock, 3rd C Battalion.
W. E. H. Martin, 3rd C Battalion.
S. F. Meiklejohn, 3rd C Battalion.

The North Auckland Regiment.

Mark de Renzie Petrie to be 2nd Lieutenant, 1st Battalion. Dated 29th November, 1927.

The undermentioned to be 2nd Lieutenants, and are seconded for duty with the 2nd C Battalion. Dated 30th November, 1927.

John Adrian Speer.
William John Bishop Speer.

The Hauraki Regiment.

The undermentioned to be 2nd Lieutenants, 1st Battalion. Dated 30th November, 1927.

Thomas Ralph Birdsall.
Norman Allan Corcoran.
Rowland Jones.
Clarence Thomas James Luxton.
George Edwin Wilkins.
John Harry Thomas.
Norman William Steele.
Alan Joseph Boyd Dixon.

The Hawke's Bay Regiment.

Lieutenant E. S. West, 1st C Battalion, is transferred to the Reserve of Officers, Class I (*b*), R.D. 7. Dated 2nd December, 1927.

The undermentioned to be 2nd Lieutenants. Dated 13th September, 1927.

Vernon D'Arcy Blackburn, 1st Battalion.
Robert Blair Schulze, and seconded for duty with the 3rd C Battalion.
Thomas Philip Lewis Reaney, and seconded for duty with the 2nd C Battalion.
John Stanley Shirley, and seconded for duty with the 2nd C Battalion.
William John Herlihy, 1st Battalion.
Henry Symes Budd, and seconded for duty with the 2nd C Battalion.
Frederick Daniel Lewis, 1st Battalion.
Frank Leonard Heaton, and seconded for duty with the 2nd C Battalion.
Frederick Alfred John Goodall, 1st Battalion.
Stuart James Kernan Hislop, and seconded for duty with the 2nd C Battalion.
William Henry Thodey, and seconded for duty with the 4th C Battalion.
Hunter George Witters, and seconded for duty with the 4th C Battalion.

The Canterbury Regiment.

The undermentioned Lieutenants to be Captains. Dated 1st December, 1927.

J. Burns, 4th C Battalion.
T. H. Mitchell, 4th C Battalion.
J. B. McBride, 3rd C Battalion.

The Otago Regiment.

The undermentioned Lieutenants to be Captains.

G. Swan, *M.C.*, 1st Battalion. Dated 15th September, 1927.
J. A. McL. Roy, *M.C.*, 1st Battalion. Dated 15th September, 1927.
A. C. Swanson, 2nd C Battalion. Dated 16th September, 1927.
R. S. Orr, 1st Battalion. Dated 16th September, 1927.
R. J. Rutherford, 2nd C Battalion. Dated 16th September, 1927.
Lieutenant J. J. Kernohan, 1st Battalion, is granted the temporary rank of Captain. Dated 2nd December, 1927.

The Southland Regiment.

Lieutenant A. R. C. Smart, from the Reserve of Officers, to be Lieutenant, 1st Battalion. Dated 30th November, 1927.

N.Z. AIR FORCE.

Arthur Hubert Keene to be 2nd Lieutenant (*on probation*). Dated 1st December, 1927.

F. J. ROLLESTON, Minister of Defence.

No.

MINUTE SHEET.

For Gazette.

The Canterbury Regiment

Lieutenant J. B. McBride, 3rd C. Battalion, to be Captain. Dated 1st December 1927.

3/12/27.

R. Smythe Lieut-Col.
Adjutant General.

2592

[N.Z.—199.

Examination for Promotion of Officers in the New Zealand Territorial Force.

General Headquarters,

Wellington, 20th April, 1926

I am directed to inform you that the marks you obtained at the examination held in February, 1926 are as follows:—

—	B 1 or D 1.	B 2 or D 2.	B 3 or D 3.	B/O or D	Total.	E.	E.	E.	Tactical Fitness, Part II.	
Maximum, 200 ...									Maximum, 300 ...	
Required to pass, 100									Req. to pass, 180	
Marks obtained ...	110	139	119	114	482	----	----	----	Marks obtained...	

You have been recorded as having qualified in Examination B for Promotion to the rank of Captain

Index No. 94

Rank and name: Lieutenant McBride, J.B.

Unit: 3rd C. Bn. Canterbury Regiment.

R. Conway Capt G.S. for, Colonel,
Chief of the General Staff.

NEW ZEALAND MILITARY FORCES.

MILITARY EXAMINATIONS.

RESULT of EXAMINATION for PROMOTION of an OFFICER of the NEW ZEALAND MILITARY FORCES.

Place and Date of Examination	Rank at Date of Examination	Name in full, and Unit	Rank for which examined	Result and Remarks
CHRISTCHURCH 17. 2. 1926	Lieutenant	McBride, Joseph Bell 3rd C.Bn., Canterbury Rgt.	Captain	passed.

Wellington, 15th April, 1926.

Colonel,
Chief of the General St

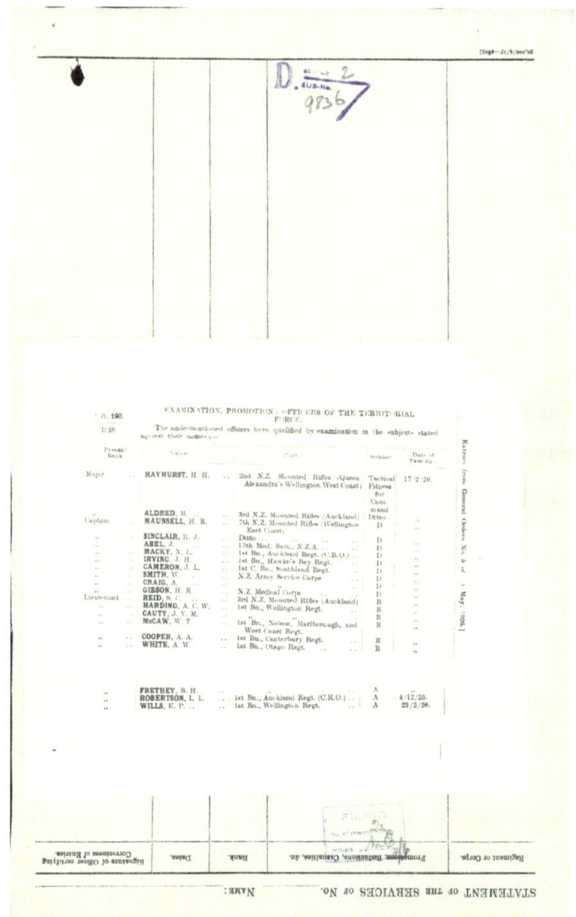

D. 9836

G.O. 190.
1/26

EXAMINATION, PROMOTION: OFFICERS OF THE TERRITORIAL FORCE.

The undermentioned officers have qualified by examination in the subjects stated against their names:—

Present Rank	Name	Unit	Subject	Date of Passing
Major	HAYHURST, H. H.	2nd N.Z. Mounted Rifles (Queen Alexandra's Wellington West Coast)	Tactical Fitness for Command	17/2/26.
"	ALDRED, M.	3rd N.Z. Mounted Rifles (Auckland)	Ditto	"
Captain	MAUNSELL, H. B.	7th N.Z. Mounted Rifles (Wellington East Coast)	D	"
"	SINCLAIR, R. J.	Ditto	D	"
"	ABEL, J.	15th Med. Batt., N.Z.A.	D	"
"	MACKY, N. L.	1st Bn., Auckland Regt. (C.R.O.)	D	"
"	IRVING, J. H.	1st Bn., Hawke's Bay Regt.	D	"
"	CAMERON, J. L.	1st C. Bn., Southland Regt.	D	"
"	SMITH, W.	N.Z. Army Service Corps	D	"
"	CRAIG, A.	"	D	"
"	GIBSON, H. R.	N.Z. Medical Corps	D	"
Lieutenant	REID, S. C.	3rd N.Z. Mounted Rifles (Auckland)	B	"
"	HARDING, A. C. W.	1st Bn., Wellington Regt.	B	"
"	CAUTY, J. V. M.	" "	B	"
"	McCAW, W. T.	1st Bn., Nelson, Marlborough, and West Coast Regt.	B	"
"	COOPER, A. A.	1st Bn., Canterbury Regt.	B	"
"	WHITE, A. W.	1st Bn., Otago Regt.	B	"
"	FRETHEY, B. H.	"	A	"
"	ROBERTSON, L. L.	1st Bn., Auckland Regt. (C.R.O.)	A	4/12/25.
"	WILLS, E. P.	1st Bn., Wellington Regt.	A	23/2/26.

Extract from General Orders No. 5 of May, 1926.

Regiment or Corps.	Promotions, Reductions, Casualties, &c.	Rank.	Dates.	Signature of Officer certifying Correctness of Entries.

STATEMENT of the SERVICES of No. NAME:

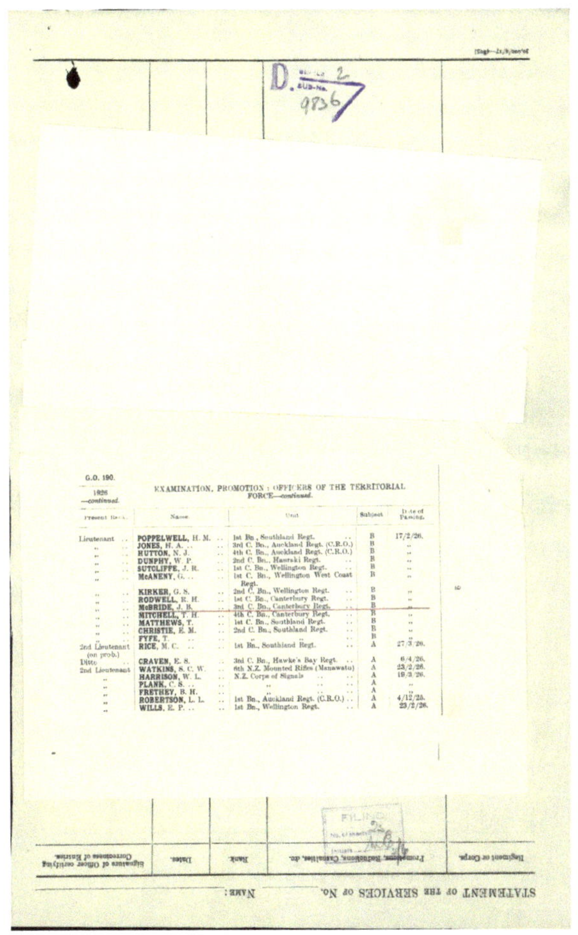

G.O. 190.

1926 —*continued.*

EXAMINATION, PROMOTION: OFFICERS OF THE TERRITORIAL FORCE—*continued.*

Present Rank.	Name.	Unit.	Subject.	Date of Passing.
Lieutenant ..	**POPPELWELL**, H. M. ..	1st Bn., Southland Regt. ..	B	17/2/26.
" ..	**JONES**, H. A.	3rd C. Bn., Auckland Regt. (C.R.O.)	B	"
" ..	**HUTTON**, N. J. ..	4th C. Bn., Auckland Regt. (C.R.O.)	B	"
" ..	**DUNPHY**, W. P. ..	2nd C. Bn., Hauraki Regt. ..	B	"
" ..	**SUTCLIFFE**, J. R. ..	1st C. Bn., Wellington Regt. ..	B	"
" ..	**McANENY**, G.	1st C. Bn., Wellington West Coast Regt.	B	"
" ..	**KIRKER**, G. S. ..	2nd C. Bn., Wellington Regt. ..	B	"
" ..	**RODWELL**, R. H. ..	1st C. Bn., Canterbury Regt. ..	B	"
" ..	**McBRIDE**, J. B. ..	3rd C. Bn., Canterbury Regt. ..	B	"
" ..	**MITCHELL**, T. H. ..	4th C. Bn., Canterbury Regt. ..	B	"
" ..	**MATTHEWS**, T. ..	1st C. Bn., Southland Regt. ..	B	"
" ..	**CHRISTIE**, E. M. ..	2nd C. Bn., Southland Regt. ..	B	"
" ..	**FYFE**, T.	" " ..	B	"
2nd Lieutenant (on prob.)	**RICE**, M. C.	1st Bn., Southland Regt. ..	A	27/3/26.
Ditto ..	**CRAVEN**, E. S. ..	3rd C. Bn., Hawke's Bay Regt. ..	A	6/4/26.
2nd Lieutenant	**WATKINS**, S. C. W. ..	6th N.Z. Mounted Rifles (Manawatu)	A	23/2/26.
"	**HARRISON**, W. L. ..	N.Z. Corps of Signals	A	19/3/26.
"	**PLANK**, C. S.	"	A	"
"	**FRETHEY**, B. H. ..	"	A	"
"	**ROBERTSON**, L. L. ..	1st Bn., Auckland Regt. (C.R.O.) ..	A	4/12/25.
"	**WILLS**, E. P.	1st Bn., Wellington Regt. ..	A	23/2/26.

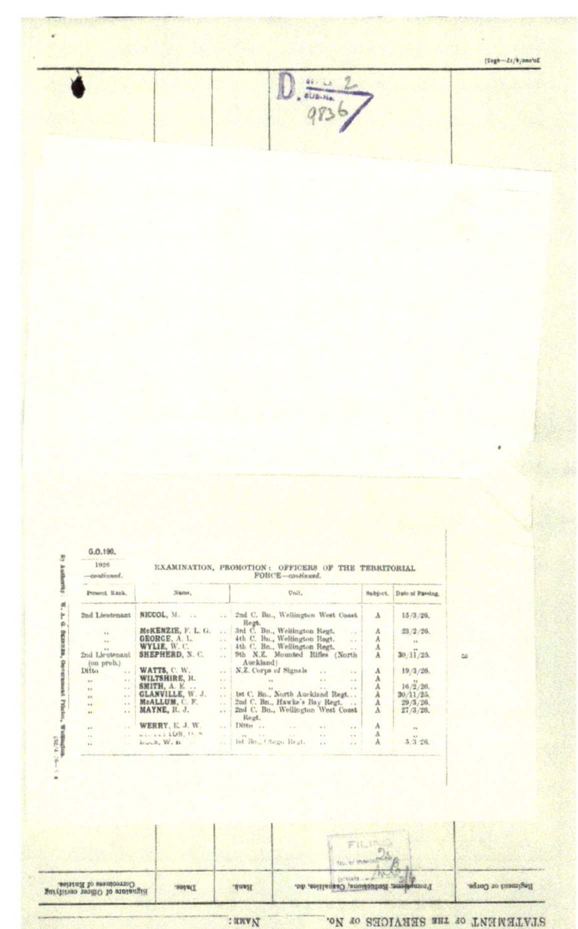

G.O.190.

1926 —*continued.*

EXAMINATION, PROMOTION: OFFICERS OF THE TERRITORIAL FORCE—*continued.*

Present Rank.	Name.	Unit.	Subject.	Date of Passing.
2nd Lieutenant	**NICCOL**, M.	2nd C. Bn., Wellington West Coast Regt.	A	15/3/26.
"	**McKENZIE**, F. L. G. ..	3rd C. Bn., Wellington Regt. ..	A	23/2/26.
"	**GEORGE**, A. L. ..	4th C. Bn., Wellington Regt. ..	A	"
"	**WYLIE**, W. C. ..	4th C. Bn., Wellington Regt. ..	A	"
2nd Lieutenant (on prob.)	**SHEPHERD**, N. C. ..	9th N.Z. Mounted Rifles (North Auckland)	A	30/11/25.
Ditto ..	**WATTS**, C. W. ..	N.Z. Corps of Signals	A	19/3/26.
" ..	**WILTSHIRE**, R. ..	"	A	"
" ..	**SMITH**, A. E.	"	A	16/2/26.
" ..	**GLANVILLE**, W. J. ..	1st C. Bn., North Auckland Regt. ..	A	30/11/25.
" ..	**McALLUM**, C. F. ..	2nd C. Bn., Hawke's Bay Regt. ..	A	29/3/26.
" ..	**MAYNE**, R. J. ..	2nd C. Bn., Wellington West Coast Regt.	A	27/3/26.
" ..	**WERRY**, E. J. W. ..	Ditto	A	"
" ..	[illegible] ..	"	A	"
" ..	...S, W. H. ..	1st Bn., Otago Regt.	A	5/3/26.

By Authority: W. A. G. Skinner, Government Printer, Wellington.

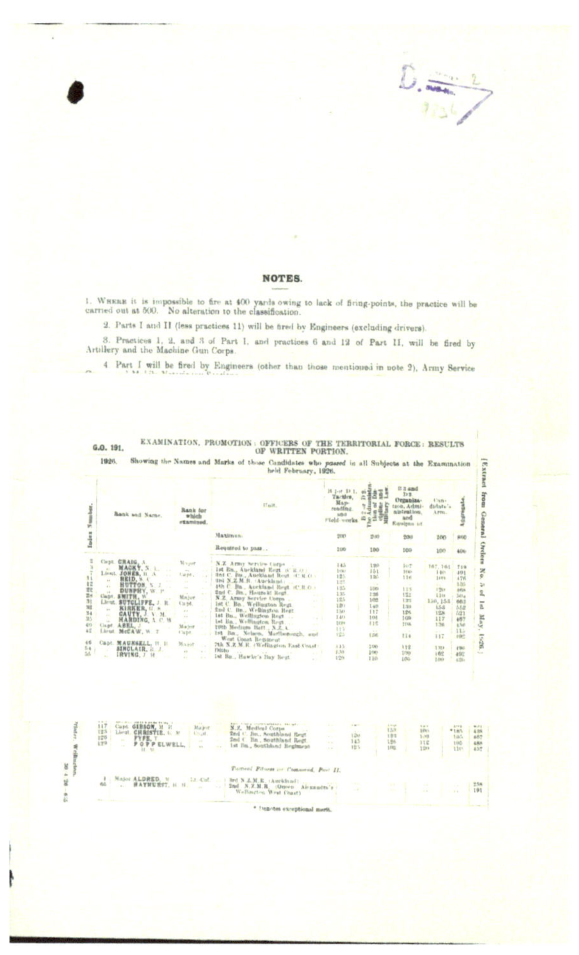

NOTES.

1. Where it is impossible to fire at 400 yards owing to lack of firing-points, the practice will be carried out at 500. No alteration to the classification.

2. Parts I and II (less practices 11) will be fired by Engineers (excluding drivers).

3. Practices 1, 2, and 3 of Part I, and practices 6 and 12 of Part II, will be fired by Artillery and the Machine Gun Corps.

4. Part I will be fired by Engineers (other than those mentioned in note 2), Army Service

G.O. 191. EXAMINATION, PROMOTION: OFFICERS OF THE TERRITORIAL FORCE: RESULTS OF WRITTEN PORTION.

1926. Showing the Names and Marks of those Candidates who *passed* in all Subjects at the Examination held February, 1926.

Index Number.	Rank and Name.	Rank for which examined.	Unit.	B 1 or D 1. Tactics, Map-reading and Field-works	B 2 or D 2. The Administration of Discipline and Military Law.	B 3 and D 3 Organisation, Administration, and Equipment	Candidate's Arm.	Aggregate.
			Maximum	200	200	200	200	800
			Required to pass ..	100	100	100	100	400
2	Capt. CRAIG, A.	Major	N.Z. Army Service Corps	145	120	107	167, 161	719
3	.. MACKY, N. L.	—	1st Bn., Auckland Regt (C.R.O.)	100	151	100	140	491
7	Lieut. JONES, H. A.	Capt.	3rd C. Bn., Auckland Regt (C.R.O.)	125	125	116	109	476
11	.. REID, R. C.	..	3rd N.Z.M.R. (Auckland)	125				
12	.. HUTTON, N. J.	..	4th C. Bn., Auckland Regt (C.R.O.)					135
22	.. DUNPHY, W. P.	..	2nd C. Bn., Hauraki Regt	125	100	113	120	468
28	Capt. SMITH, W.	Major	N.Z. Army Service Corps	135	126	122	110	504
31	Lieut. SUTCLIFFE, J. R.	Capt.	1st C. Bn., Wellington Regt	125	102	133	150, 153	663
32	.. KIRKER, G. S.	..	2nd C. Bn., Wellington Regt	120	140	130	153	552
34	.. CAUTY, J. V. M.	..	1st Bn., Wellington Regt	150	117	126	128	521
35	.. HARDING, A. C. W.	..	1st Bn., Wellington Regt	140	101	109	117	467
40	Capt. ABEL, J.	Major	19th Medium Batt., N.Z.A.	109	115	108	126	456
42	Lieut. McCAW, W. T.	Capt.	1st Bn., Nelson, Marlborough, and West Coast Regiment	115 / 125	126	114	117	115 / 492
46	Capt. MAUNSELL, H. H.	Major	7th N.Z.M.R. (Wellington East Coast)	115	100	112	130	496
54	.. SINCLAIR, R. J.	..	Ditto	130	100	100	162	492
56	.. IRVING, J. H.	..	1st Bn., Hawke's Bay Regt	120	110	100	100	430
117	Capt. GIBSON, M. R.	Major	N.Z. Medical Corps		153	100	*185	438
123	Lieut. CHRISTIE, E. M.	Capt.	2nd C. Bn., Southland Regt	120	133	109	165	467
126	.. FYFE, T.	..	2nd C. Bn., Southland Regt	145	126	112	105	488
129	.. POPPELWELL, H. M.	..	1st Bn., Southland Regiment	125	102	120	110	457

Tactical Fitness for Command, Part II.

Index Number.	Rank and Name.	Rank for which examined.	Unit.					Aggregate.
1	Major ALDRED, M.	Lt.-Col.	3rd N.Z.M.R. (Auckland)	..	..	..	..	258
66	.. HAYHURST, H. H.	..	2nd N.Z.M.R. (Queen Alexandra's Wellington West Coast)	..	..	..	..	191

* Denotes exceptional merit.

[Extract from General Orders No. 5 of 1st May, 1926.]

Printer, Wellington.

30 4 26—6.5

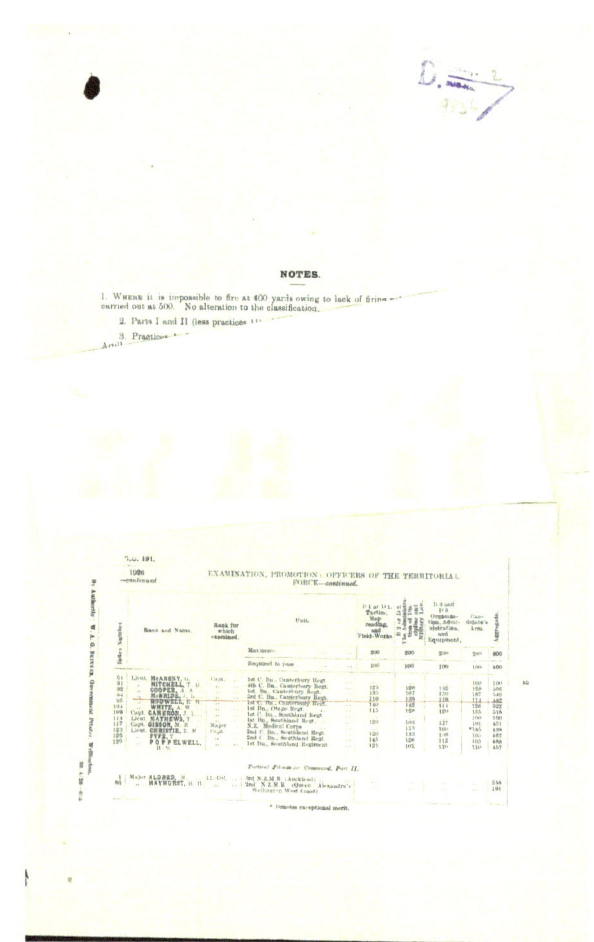

NOTES.

1. Where it is impossible to fire at 400 yards owing to lack of firin... carried out at 500. No alteration to the classification.

2. Parts I and II (less practices ...

3. Practice...

G.O. 191.

1926 —*continued.* EXAMINATION, PROMOTION: OFFICERS OF THE TERRITORIAL FORCE—*continued.*

Index Number.	Rank and Name.	Rank for which examined.	Unit.	B 1 or D 1. Tactics, Map-reading, and Field-Works.	B 2 or D 2. The Administration of Discipline and Military Law.	B 3 and D 3 Organisation, Administration, and Equipment.	Candidate's Arm.	Aggregate.
			Maximum	200	200	200	200	800
			Required to pass	100	100	100	100	400
61	Lieut. McANENY, G.	Capt.	1st C. Bn., Canterbury Regt	..	..	..	100	100
91	.. MITCHELL, T. H.	..	4th C. Bn., Canterbury Regt.	125	120	132	129	506
92	.. COOPER, A. A.	..	1st. Bn., Canterbury Regt.	135	107	130	167	549
94	.. McBRIDE, J. L.	..	3rd C. Bn., Canterbury Regt.	110	139	119	114	482
95	.. RODWELL, E. H.	..	1st C. Bn., Canterbury Regt.	140	142	114	126	522
104	.. WHITE, A. W.	..	1st Bn., Otago Regt	115	128	120	155	518
109	Capt. CAMERON, J. L.	..	1st C. Bn., Southland Regt.	..	..	..	100	100
114	Lieut. MATHEWS, T.	..	1st Bn., Southland Regt.	120	103	127	101	451
117	Capt. GIBSON, M. R.	Major	N.Z. Medical Corps	..	113	100	*185	438
123	Lieut. CHRISTIE, E. M.	Capt.	2nd C. Bn., Southland Regt.	120	133	109	165	467
126	.. FYFE, T.	..	2nd C. Bn., Southland Regt.	145	126	112	103	488
129	.. POPPELWELL, H. M.	..	1st Bn., Southland Regiment	125	102	120	110	457

Tactical Fitness for Command, Part II.

Index Number.	Rank and Name.	Rank for which examined.	Unit.					Aggregate.
1	Major ALDRED, M.	Lt.-Col.	3rd N.Z.M.R. (Auckland)	..	..	..	..	258
66	.. HAYHURST, H. H.	..	2nd N.Z.M.R. (Queen Alexandra's Wellington West Coast)	..	..	..	..	191

* Denotes exceptional merit.

By Authority: W. A. G. Skinner, Government Printer, Wellington.

30 4 26—6.5

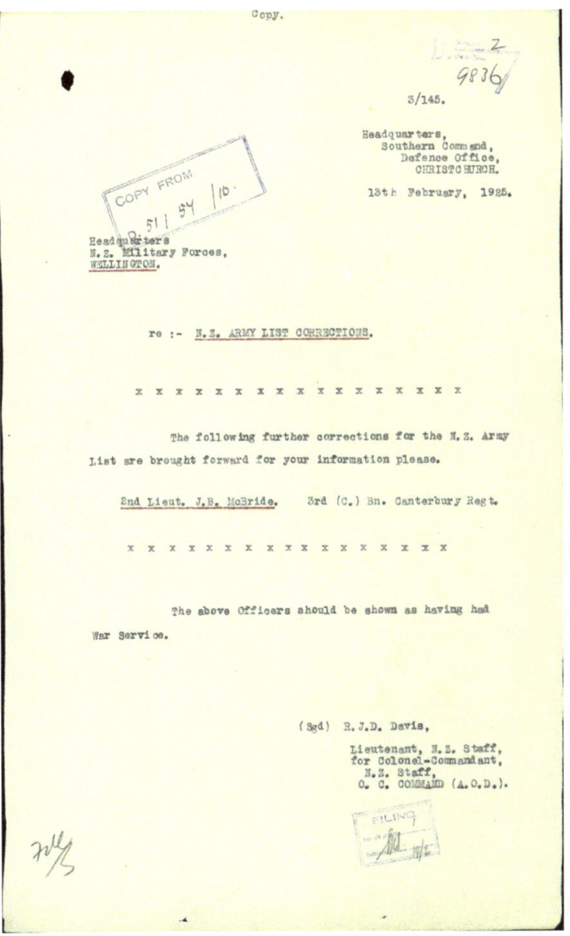

Copy.

3/145.

Headquarters,
Southern Command,
Defence Office,
CHRISTCHURCH.

13th February, 1925.

COPY FROM 51/54/10.

Headquarters
N.Z. Military Forces,
WELLINGTON.

re :- N.Z. ARMY LIST CORRECTIONS.

x x x x x x x x x x x x x x x x x

The following further corrections for the N.Z. Army List are brought forward for your information please.

2nd Lieut. J.B. McBride. 3rd (C.) Bn. Canterbury Regt.

x x x x x x x x x x x x x x x x x

The above Officers should be shown as having had War Service.

(Sgd) R.J.D. Davis,
Lieutenant, N.Z. Staff,
for Colonel-Commandant,
N.Z. Staff,
O. C. COMMAND (A.O.D.).

FILING

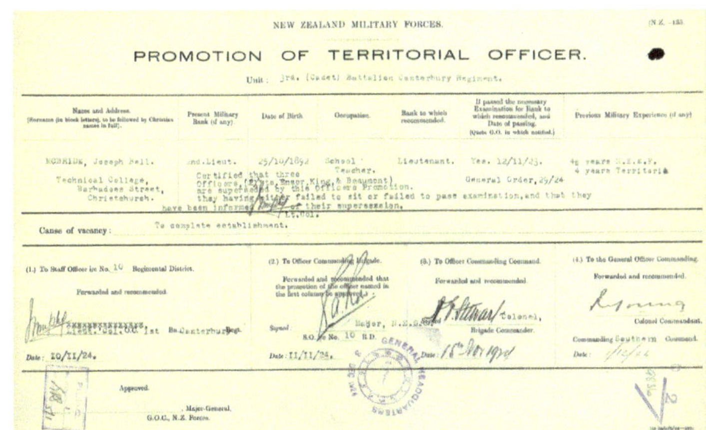

NEW ZEALAND MILITARY FORCES. (N.Z. -135)

PROMOTION OF TERRITORIAL OFFICER.

Unit: 3rd. (Cadet) Battalion Canterbury Regiment.

Name and Address. (Surname (in block letters), to be followed by Christian names in full).	Present Military Rank (if any).	Date of Birth.	Occupation.	Rank to which recommended.	If passed the necessary Examination for Rank to which recommended, and Date of passing. (Quote G.O. in which notified.)	Previous Military Experience (if any).
MCBRIDE, Joseph Bell. Technical College, Barbadoes Street, Christchurch.	2nd.Lieut.	25/10/1892	School Teacher.	Lieutenant.	Yes. 12/11/23. General Order, 29/24	4½ years N.Z.E.F. 4 years Territorial

Certified that three Officers, (2/Lts. Enser, King, & Beaumont) are superseded by this Officers Promotion. they having either failed to sit or failed to pass examination, and that they have been informed of their supersession.
Lt.Col.

Cause of vacancy: To complete establishment.

(1.) To Staff Officer i/c No. 10 Regimental District.
Forwarded and recommended.
Lieut.-Col. O.C. 1st Bn. Canterbury Regt.
Date: 10/11/24.

(2.) To Officer Commanding Brigade.
Forwarded and recommended that the promotion of the officer named in the first column be approved.
Signed: Major, N.Z.S.C.
S.O. i/c No. 10 R.D.
Date: 11/11/24.

(3.) To Officer Commanding Command.
Forwarded and recommended.
Signed: Colonel,
Brigade Commander.
Date: 15th Nov 1924

(4.) To the General Officer Commanding.
Forwarded and recommended.
Colonel Commandant.
Commanding Southern Command.
Date: 1/12/24

Approved.
, Major-General.
G.O.C., N.Z. Forces.
Date:

GENERAL HEADQUARTERS

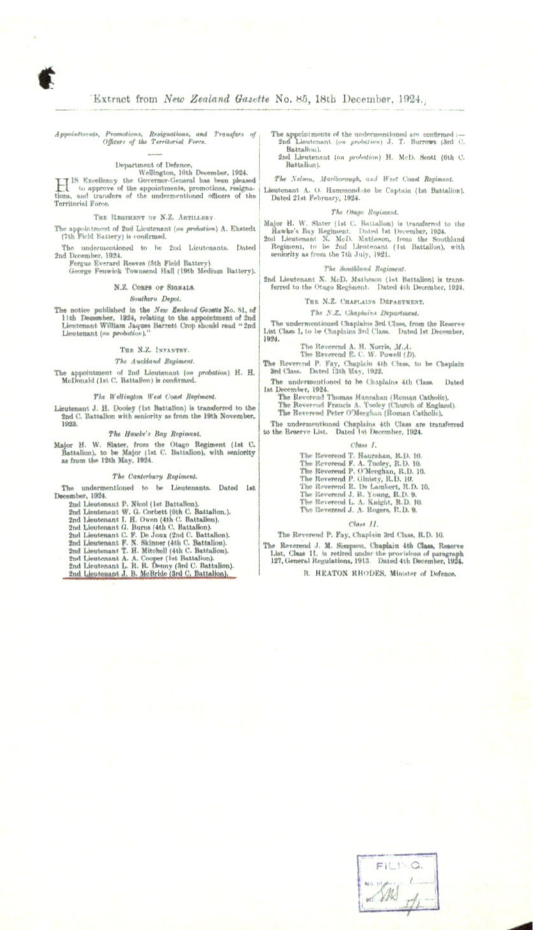

Extract from *New Zealand Gazette* No. 85, 18th December, 1924.

Appointments, Promotions, Resignations, and Transfers of Officers of the Territorial Force.

Department of Defence,
Wellington, 10th December, 1924.

HIS Excellency the Governor-General has been pleased to approve of the appointments, promotions, resignations, and transfers of the undermentioned officers of the Territorial Force.

THE REGIMENT OF N.Z. ARTILLERY.

The appointment of 2nd Lieutenant (*on probation*) A. Ekstedt (7th Field Battery) is confirmed.

The undermentioned to be 2nd Lieutenants. Dated 2nd December, 1924.

Fergus Everard Reeves (5th Field Battery).
George Fenwick Townsend Hall (19th Medium Battery).

N.Z. CORPS OF SIGNALS.

Southern Depot.

The notice published in the *New Zealand Gazette* No. 81, of 11th December, 1924, relating to the appointment of 2nd Lieutenant William Jaques Barrett Crop should read "2nd Lieutenant (*on probation*)."

THE N.Z. INFANTRY.

The Auckland Regiment.

The appointment of 2nd Lieutenant (*on probation*) H. H. McDonald (1st C. Battalion) is confirmed.

The Wellington West Coast Regiment.

Lieutenant J. H. Dooley (1st Battalion) is transferred to the 2nd C. Battalion with seniority as from the 19th November, 1923.

The Hawke's Bay Regiment.

Major H. W. Slater, from the Otago Regiment (1st C. Battalion), to be Major (1st C. Battalion), with seniority as from the 12th May, 1924.

The Canterbury Regiment.

The undermentioned to be Lieutenants. Dated 1st December, 1924.

2nd Lieutenant P. Nicol (1st Battalion).
2nd Lieutenant W. G. Corbett (6th C. Battalion.).
2nd Lieutenant I. H. Owen (4th C. Battalion).
2nd Lieutenant G. Burns (4th C. Battalion).
2nd Lieutenant C. F. De Joux (2nd C. Battalion).
2nd Lieutenant F. N. Skinner (4th C. Battalion).
2nd Lieutenant T. H. Mitchell (4th C. Battalion).
2nd Lieutenant A. A. Cooper (1st Battalion).
2nd Lieutenant L. R. R. Denny (3rd C. Battalion).
2nd Lieutenant J. B. McBride (3rd C. Battalion).

The appointments of the undermentioned are confirmed :—

2nd Lieutenant (*on probation*) J. T. Burrows (3rd C. Battalion).
2nd Lieutenant (*on probation*) H. McD. Scott (6th C. Battalion).

The Nelson, Marlborough, and West Coast Regiment.

Lieutenant A. O. Hammond to be Captain (1st Battalion). Dated 21st February, 1924.

The Otago Regiment.

Major H. W. Slater (1st C. Battalion) is transferred to the Hawke's Bay Regiment. Dated 1st December, 1924.

2nd Lieutenant N. McD. Matheson, from the Southland Regiment, to be 2nd Lieutenant (1st Battalion), with seniority as from the 7th July, 1921.

The Southland Regiment.

2nd Lieutenant N. McD. Matheson (1st Battalion) is transferred to the Otago Regiment. Dated 4th December, 1924.

THE N.Z. CHAPLAINS DEPARTMENT.

The N.Z. Chaplains Department.

The undermentioned Chaplains 3rd Class, from the Reserve List Class I, to be Chaplains 3rd Class. Dated 1st December, 1924.

The Reverend A. H. Norris, *M.A.*
The Reverend E. C. W. Powell (*D*).

The Reverend P. Fay, Chaplain 4th Class, to be Chaplain 3rd Class. Dated 12th May, 1922.

The undermentioned to be Chaplains 4th Class. Dated 1st December, 1924.

The Reverend Thomas Hanrahan (Roman Catholic).
The Reverend Francis A. Tooley (Church of England).
The Reverend Peter O'Meeghan (Roman Catholic).

The undermentioned Chaplains 4th Class are transferred to the Reserve List. Dated 1st December, 1924.

Class I.

The Reverend T. Hanrahan, R.D. 10.
The Reverend F. A. Tooley, R.D. 10.
The Reverend P. O'Meeghan, R.D. 10.
The Reverend P. Ginisty, R.D. 10.
The Reverend R. De Lambert, R.D. 10.
The Reverend J. R. Young, R.D. 9.
The Reverend L. A. Knight, R.D. 10.
The Reverend J. A. Rogers, R.D. 9.

Class II.

The Reverend P. Fay, Chaplain 3rd Class, R.D. 10.

The Reverend J. M. Simpson, Chaplain 4th Class, Reserve List, Class II, is retired under the provisions of paragraph 127, General Regulations, 1913. Dated 4th December, 1924.

R. HEATON RHODES, Minister of Defence.

No. **MINUTE SHEET.**

For Gazette.

The Canterbury Regiment

2nd Lieutenant J. B. McBride to be Lieutenant (3rd C. Battalion). Dated 1st December 1924.

3/12/24. R H Smythe

~~Delay Gazette pending enquiry~~ RHS 4/12/24

NEW ZEALAND MILITARY FORCES

17/24/10

Headquarters,
Southern Command,
Christchurch.

5th November, 1924.

Headquarters,
1st Bn. Canterbury Regiment,
CHRISTCHURCH.

PROMOTION OF OFFICERS - CANTERBURY REGIMENT.

Forms for promotion of the following officers of your unit have been received in this office and are returned herewith.-

2/Lieut. I.S. Owen, 4th (R) Bn. Canterbury Regiment
" G. Burns. " " " " "
" F.E. Skinner. " " " " "
" T.H. Mitchell " " " " "
" L.H.S. Denny. 3rd " " " "
" J.D. McBride " " " " "

The promotion of these officers will cause the supersession of the following.-

ø 2/Lieut. F.H. Wilson x " J. Nicol " A.G. Gurnsey " L.LeF. Knecr " W.G. Corbett " C.L. King	will be superseded by 2/Lieuts. Owen and Burns.
The above and 2/Lieut. L.E. Galbraith x " C.F. de Joux	will be superseded by 2/Lieuts. Skinner and Mitchell
The above and 2/Lieut. R.S. Beaumont x " A.A. Cowper	will be superseded by 2/Lieuts Denny and McBride

ø This officer is in course of transfer to the Reserve.

x These officers have passed their "A" Examination and are therefore also qualified for promotion.

I shall be glad if you will have Forms N.Z.137 (copy attached) completed in duplicate in the case of the officers recommended for promotion and specify thereon the names and the reasons for the supersession of the officers concerned, and a certificate should also be endorsed to the effect that all the

(2)

officers being superseded have been notified, vide this office memorandum 17/24/10 of the 11th ultimo.

Major, N.Z. Staff,
A.A. & Q.M.G.,
SOUTHERN COMMAND.

Enclo/

Copy to Area 10A, Chch.

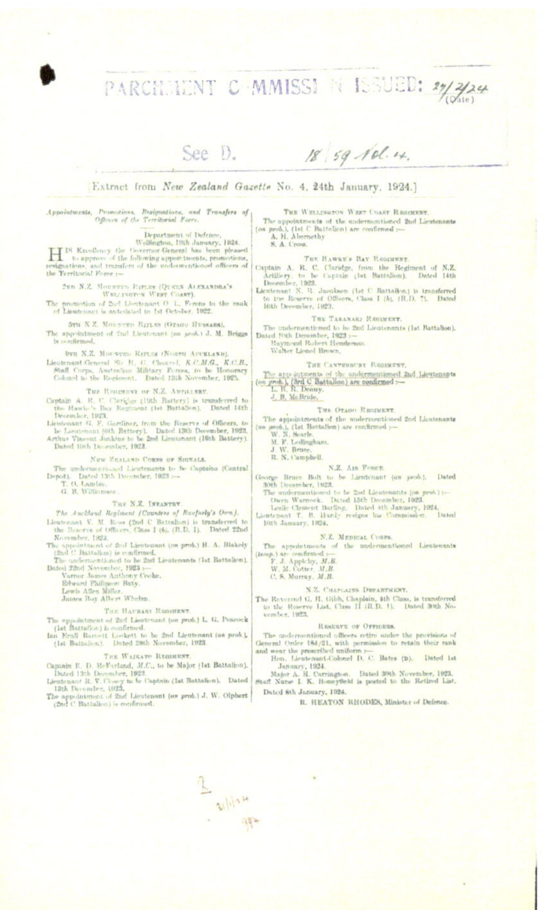

PARCHMENT C MMISSI N ISSUED: 27/2/24
(Date)

See D. 18/59 Vol. 4.

[Extract from *New Zealand Gazette* No. 4, 24th January, 1924.]

Appointments, Promotions, Resignations, and Transfers of Officers of the Territorial Force.

Department of Defence,
Wellington, 19th January, 1924.

HIS Excellency the Governor-General has been pleased to approve of the following appointments, promotions, resignations, and transfers of the undermentioned officers of the Territorial Force :—

2ND N.Z. MOUNTED RIFLES (QUEEN ALEXANDRA'S WELLINGTON WEST COAST).

The promotion of 2nd Lieutenant O. L. Ferens to the rank of Lieutenant is antedated to 1st October, 1922.

5TH N.Z. MOUNTED RIFLES (OTAGO HUSSARS).

The appointment of 2nd Lieutenant (*on prob.*) J. M. Briggs is confirmed.

9TH N.Z. MOUNTED RIFLES (NORTH AUCKLAND).

Lieutenant-General Sir H. G. Chauvel, *K.C.M.G.*, *K.C.B.*, Staff Corps, Australian Military Forces, to be Honorary Colonel to the Regiment. Dated 13th November, 1923.

THE REGIMENT OF N.Z. ARTILLERY.

Captain A. R. C. Claridge (19th Battery) is transferred to the Hawke's Bay Regiment (1st Battalion). Dated 14th December, 1923.

Lieutenant G. F. Gardiner, from the Reserve of Officers, to be Lieutenant (6th Battery). Dated 13th December, 1923.

Arthur Vincent Jenkins to be 2nd Lieutenant (19th Battery). Dated 10th December, 1923.

NEW ZEALAND CORPS OF SIGNALS.

The undermentioned Lieutenants to be Captains (Central Depot). Dated 13th December, 1923 :—
T. O. Lambie.
G. B. Williamson.

THE N.Z. INFANTRY.

The Auckland Regiment (Countess of Ranfurly's Own).

Lieutenant V. M. Ross (2nd C Battalion) is transferred to the Reserve of Officers, Class I (*b*), (R.D. 1). Dated 22nd November, 1923.

The appointment of 2nd Lieutenant (*on prob.*) H. A. Blakely (2nd C Battalion) is confirmed.

The undermentioned to be 2nd Lieutenants (1st Battalion). Dated 22nd November, 1923 :—
Varner James Anthony Cooke.
Edward Philipson Baty.
Lewis Allen Miller.
James Roy Albert Whelan.

THE HAURAKI REGIMENT.

The appointment of 2nd Lieutenant (*on prob.*) L. G. Peacock (1st Battalion) is confirmed.

Ian Ernll Barnett Lockett to be 2nd Lieutenant (*on prob.*), (1st Battalion). Dated 28th November, 1923.

THE WAIKATO REGIMENT.

Captain E. D. McFarland, *M.C.*, to be Major (1st Battalion). Dated 13th December, 1923.

Lieutenant R. V. Closey to be Captain (1st Battalion). Dated 13th December, 1923.

The appointment of 2nd Lieutenant (*on prob.*) J. W. Olphert (2nd C Battalion) is confirmed.

THE WELLINGTON WEST COAST REGIMENT.

The appointments of the undermentioned 2nd Lieutenants (*on prob.*), (1st C Battalion) are confirmed :—
A. H. Abernethy
S. A. Cross.

THE HAWKE'S BAY REGIMENT.

Captain A. R. C. Claridge, from the Regiment of N.Z. Artillery, to be Captain (1st Battalion). Dated 14th December, 1923.

Lieutenant N. R. Jacobsen (1st C Battalion) is transferred to the Reserve of Officers, Class I (*b*), (R.D. 7). Dated 10th December, 1923.

THE TARANAKI REGIMENT.

The undermentioned to be 2nd Lieutenants (1st Battalion). Dated 10th December, 1923 :—
Raymond Robert Henderson.
Walter Lionel Brown.

THE CANTERBURY REGIMENT.

The appointments of the undermentioned 2nd Lieutenants (*on prob.*), (3rd C Battalion) are confirmed :—
L. R. R. Denny.
J. B. McBride.

THE OTAGO REGIMENT.

The appointments of the undermentioned 2nd Lieutenants (*on prob.*), (1st Battalion) are confirmed :—
W. N. Searle.
M. F. Ledingham.
J. W. Bruce.
R. N. Campbell.

N.Z. AIR FORCE.

George Bruce Bolt to be Lieutenant (*on prob.*). Dated 30th December, 1923.

The undermentioned to be 2nd Lieutenants (*on prob.*) :—
Owen Warnock. Dated 15th December, 1923.
Leslie Clement Barling. Dated 4th January, 1924.

Lieutenant T. B. Hardy resigns his Commission. Dated 10th January, 1924.

N.Z. MEDICAL CORPS.

The appointments of the undermentioned Lieutenants (*temp.*) are confirmed :—
F. J. Appleby, *M.B.*
W. M. Cotter, *M.B.*
C. S. Murray, *M.B.*

N.Z. CHAPLAINS DEPARTMENT.

The Reverend G. H. Gibb, Chaplain, 4th Class, is transferred to the Reserve List, Class II (R.D. 1). Dated 30th November, 1923.

RESERVE OF OFFICERS.

The undermentioned officers retire under the provisions of General Order 184/21, with permission to retain their rank and wear the prescribed uniform :—
Hon. Lieutenant-Colonel D. C. Bates (D). Dated 1st January, 1924.
Major A. H. Carrington. Dated 30th November, 1923.

Staff Nurse I. K. Honeyfield is posted to the Retired List.

Dated 8th January, 1924.

R. HEATON RHODES, Minister of Defence.

No. **MINUTE SHEET.**

For Gazette.

The Canterbury Regiment

The appointment of 2nd Lieutenant (on prob) J. B. McBride (3rd C. Battalion) is confirmed.

14/12/23

R W Smythe

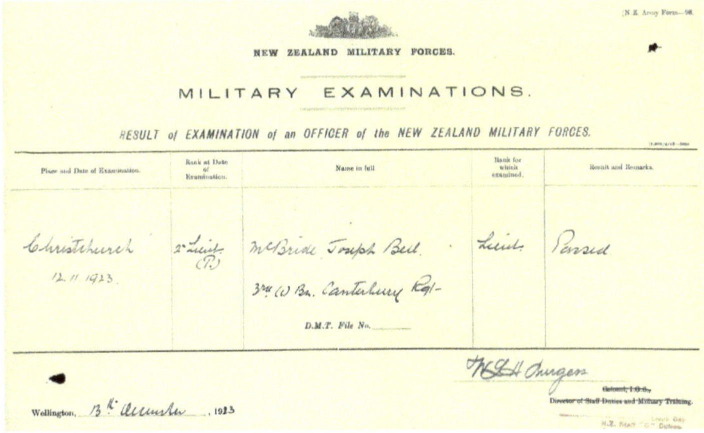

N.Z. Army Form—98.

NEW ZEALAND MILITARY FORCES.

MILITARY EXAMINATIONS.

RESULT of EXAMINATION of an OFFICER of the NEW ZEALAND MILITARY FORCES.

Place and Date of Examination.	Rank at Date of Examination.	Name in full.	Rank for which examined.	Result and Remarks.
Christchurch 12.11.1923.	2nd Lieut. (P)	McBride Joseph Bell. 3rd (C) Bn. Canterbury Regt. D.M.T. File No.	Lieut.	Passed

Colonel, I.S.C.
Director of Staff Duties and Military Training.

Wellington, 13th December, 1923

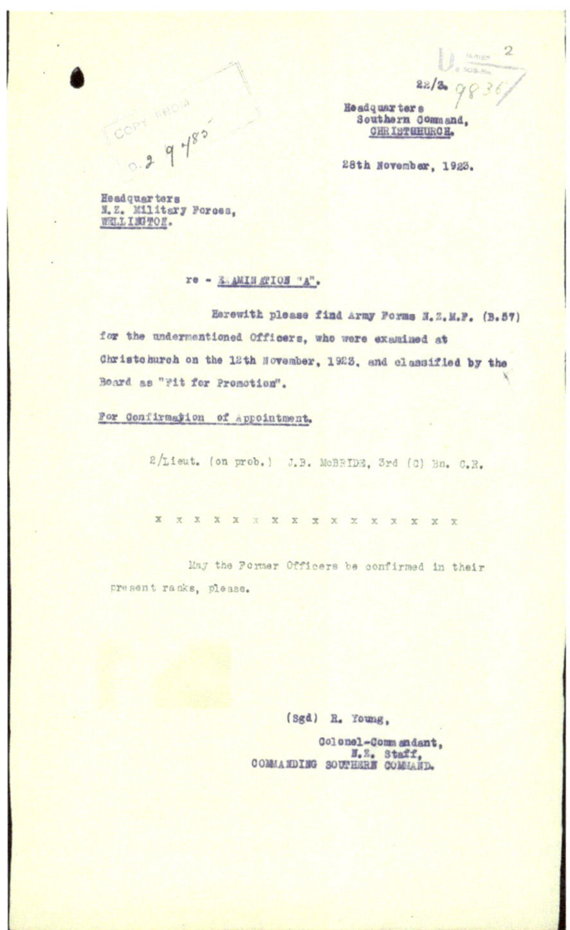

22/3. 9836

Headquarters
Southern Command,
CHRISTCHURCH.

28th November, 1923.

Headquarters
N.Z. Military Forces,
WELLINGTON.

re - EXAMINATION "A".

Herewith please find Army Forms N.Z.M.F. (B.57) for the undermentioned Officers, who were examined at Christchurch on the 12th November, 1923, and classified by the Board as "Fit for Promotion".

For Confirmation of Appointment.

2/Lieut. (on prob.) J.B. McBRIDE, 3rd (C) Bn. C.R.

x x x x x x x x x x x x x x x x

May the Former Officers be confirmed in their present ranks, please.

(Sgd) R. Young,
Colonel-Commandant,
N.Z. Staff,
COMMANDING SOUTHERN COMMAND.

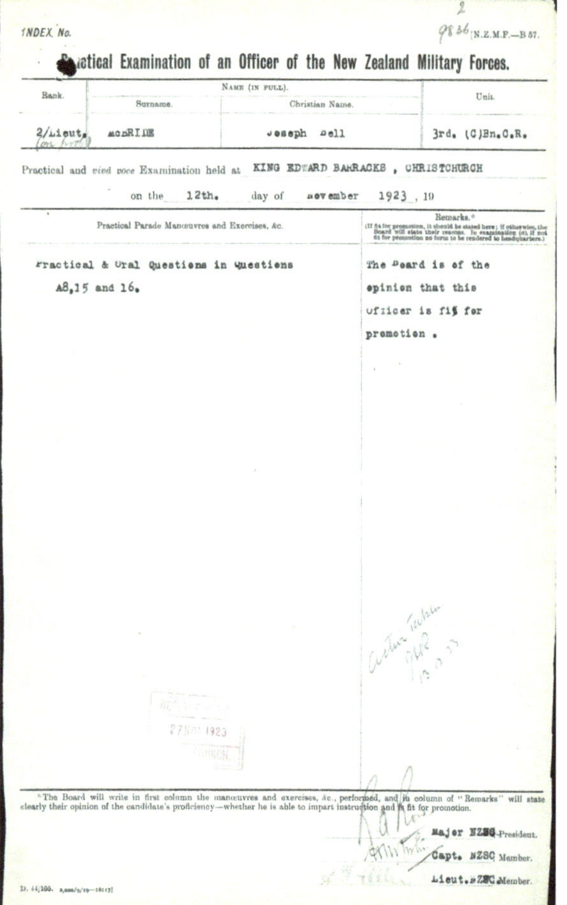

INDEX No. 9836 N.Z.M.F.—B 57.

Practical Examination of an Officer of the New Zealand Military Forces.

Rank.	Name (in full). Surname.	Christian Name.	Unit.
2/Lieut. (on prob)	McBRIDE	Joseph Bell	3rd. (C)Bn.C.R.

Practical and viva voce Examination held at KING EDWARD BARRACKS, CHRISTCHURCH on the 12th. day of November 1923, 19

Practical Parade Manœuvres and Exercises, &c.	Remarks.* (If fit for promotion, it should be stated here; if otherwise, the Board will state their reasons. In examination (a), if not fit for promotion no form to be rendered to headquarters.)
Practical & Oral Questions in Questions A8,15 and 16.	The Board is of the opinion that this Officer is fit for promotion.

*The Board will write in first column the manœuvres and exercises, &c., performed, and in column of "Remarks" will state clearly their opinion of the candidate's proficiency—whether he is able to impart instruction and is fit for promotion.

Major NZSC President.
Capt. NZSC Member.
Lieut. NZSC Member.

D. 44/100.

2
9836

[Extract from *N.Z. Gazette* No. 42, 10th May, 1923.]

Appointments, Promotions, Resignations, and Transfers of Officers of the N.Z. Staff Corps, Regiment of N.Z. Artillery, and Territorial Force.

Department of Defence,
Wellington, 9th May, 1923.

HIS Excellency the Governor-General has been pleased to approve of the appointments, promotions, resignations, and transfers of the undermentioned officers of the N.Z. Staff Corps, Regiment of Royal N.Z. Artillery, and Territorial Force.

N.Z. Staff Corps.

Lieutenant C. S. J. Duff is transferred to the Regiment of Royal N.Z. Artillery. Dated 4th May, 1923.

The Regiment of Royal N.Z. Artillery.

Lieutenant C. S. J. Duff, from the N.Z. Staff Corps, to be Lieutenant, with seniority as from the 15th December, 1920.

The Regiment of N.Z. Artillery.

2nd Lieutenant G. M. Whitaker (4th Battery) to be Lieutenant. Dated 19th April, 1923.

2nd Lieutenant H. C. Clouston (15th Battery) resigns his commission. Dated 20th April, 1923.

The N.Z. Infantry.

The Auckland Regiment.

Lieutenant W. H. Allen to be Captain (13th C. Battalion). Dated 20th April, 1923.

2nd Lieutenant W. P. Dunphy to be Lieutenant (10th C. Battalion). Dated 10th November, 1922.

Captain N. R. W. Thomas (4th Battalion) is transferred to the Reserve of Officers, Class 1 (*b*), R.D. 1. Dated 30th April, 1923.

The Wellington Regiment.

2nd Lieutenant F. H. P. Rogers, from the Otago Regiment, to be 2nd Lieutenant (4th Battalion), with seniority as from the 20th September, 1921.

The appointment of 2nd Lieutenant (*on probation*) G. McAneny (7th C. Battalion) is confirmed.

2nd Lieutenant G. F. Pealington (9th C. Battalion) is transferred to the Reserve of Officers, Class 1 (*b*), R.D. 5. Dated 20th April, 1923.

The Canterbury Regiment

The undermentioned to be 2nd Lieutenants (*on probation*), (4th C. Battalion). Dated 19th April, 1923:—

James Thomas Burrows.
Laurence Radford Ryan Denny.
Joseph Bell McBride.

The Otago Regiment.

Francis Wilkinson to be 2nd Lieutenant (*on probation*), (2nd Battalion). Dated 27th April, 1923.

2nd Lieutenant F. H. P. Rogers (2nd Battalion) is transferred to the Wellington Regiment (4th Battalion). Dated 26th April, 1923.

Captain H. S. Kenrick (1st Battalion) is transferred to the Reserve of Officers, Class 1 (*b*), R.D. 11. Dated 3rd May, 1923.

2nd Lieutenant R. Latimer (4th C. Battalion) resigns his commission. Dated 19th April, 1923.

N.Z. Medical Corps.

Colonel (*temp. Brigadier-General*) Sir D. J. McGavin, *C.M.G., D.S.O., M.D., F.R.C.S., Eng.*, Honorary Surgeon to the Governor-General to be Major-General. Dated 1st March, 1923.

Captain P. B. Benham, *M.C., M.B.*, Reserve of Officers, retires under the provisions of General Order No. 184/21 with the rank of Major, and is granted permission to wear the prescribed uniform. Dated 15th April, 1923.

Captain R. E. Paterson, Reserve of Officers, is retired under the provisions of General Order No. 184/21, with permission to retain his rank and wear the prescribed uniform. Dated 27th April, 1923.

The commission granted Captain G. W. Matthews is cancelled under section 5 (2) of the Defence Act, 1909. Dated 17th April, 1923.

R. HEATON RHODES, Minister of Defence.

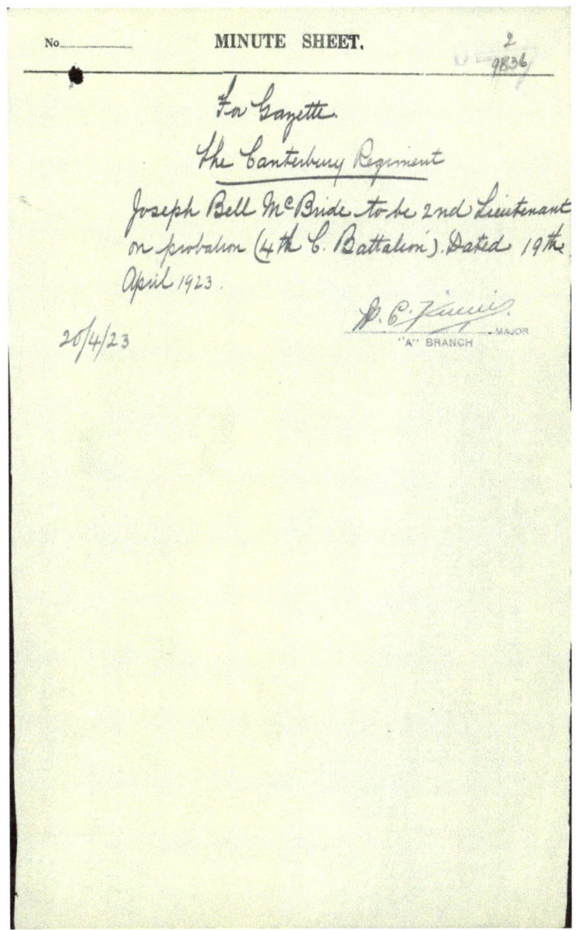

No. 2 9836

MINUTE SHEET.

For Gazette.

The Canterbury Regiment

Joseph Bell McBride to be 2nd Lieutenant on probation (4th C. Battalion). Dated 19th April 1923.

20/4/23

[signature] MAJOR
"A" BRANCH

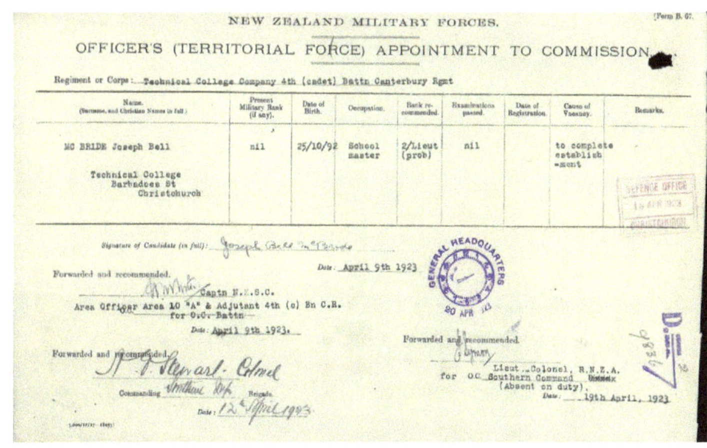

NEW ZEALAND MILITARY FORCES. (Form B. 67.

OFFICER'S (TERRITORIAL FORCE) APPOINTMENT TO COMMISSION.

Regiment or Corps: Technical College Company 4th (cadet) Battn Canterbury Rgmt

Name. (Surname, and Christian Names in full.)	Present Military Rank (if any).	Date of Birth.	Occupation.	Rank recommended.	Examinations passed.	Date of Registration.	Cause of Vacancy.	Remarks.
MC BRIDE Joseph Bell Technical College Barbadoes St Christchurch	nil	25/10/92	School master	2/Lieut (prob)	nil		to complete establish -ment	

DEFENCE OFFICE 1 APR 1923 CHRISTCHURCH

Signature of Candidate (in full): Joseph Bell McBride

Date: April 9th 1923

GENERAL HEADQUARTERS 20 APR 1923

Forwarded and recommended.

[signature] Captn N.Z.S.C.
Area Officer Area 10 "A" & Adjutant 4th (c) Bn C.R.
~~for O.C. Battn~~

Date: April 9th 1923.

Forwarded and recommended.

[signature] Lieut.-Colonel, R.N.Z.A.
for OC Southern Command
(Absent on duty).

Date: 19th April, 1923

Forwarded and recommended.

N. P. Stewart Colonel
Commanding Southern Inf Brigade.

Date: 12th April 1923

D. 9836

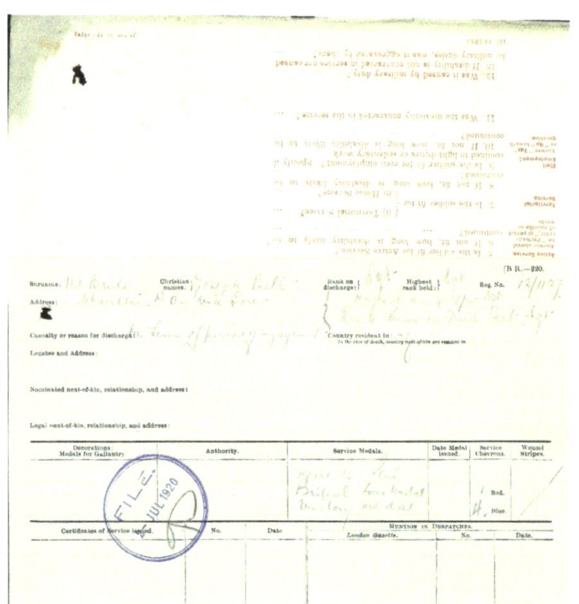

[B R.—220.

Surname: | Christian names: | Rank on discharge: | Highest rank held: | Reg. No. 12/1127

Address:

Casualty or reason for discharge:

Country resident in:
In the case of death, country next-of-kin are resident in.

Legatee and Address:

Nominated next-of-kin, relationship, and address:

Legal next-of-kin, relationship, and address:

Decorations: Medals for Gallantry	Authority.	Service Medals.	Date Medal issued.	Service Chevrons.	Wound Stripes.
		British War Medal Victory Medal		1 Red. 4 Blue.	

FILE. JUL 1920

Certificates of Service issued.	No.	Date	Mention in Despatches. London Gazette.	No.	Date.

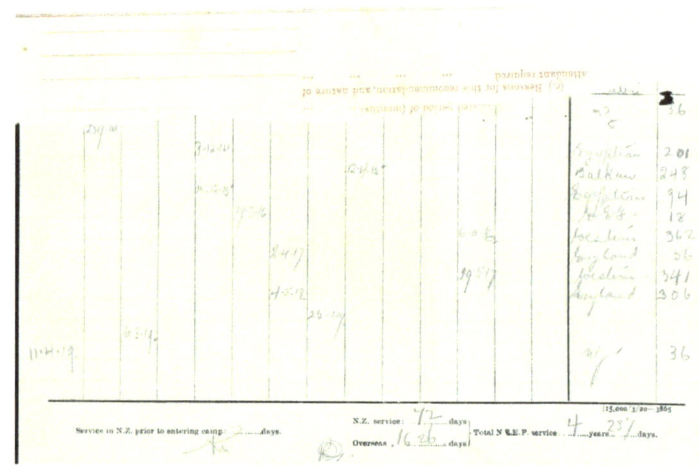

Attendant required

(c) Reasons for this recommendation and nature of

Place	Days
	36
Egyptian	201
Balkan	248
Egyptian	94
	18
Western	362
England	56
Western	341
England	306
	36

[15,000/3/20—3865

Service in N.Z. prior to entering camp: ...... days.

N.Z. service: 72 days
Overseas: 1626 days
Total N.Z.E.F. service 4 years 237 days.

Joseph served for the New Zealand Expeditionary Forces for a total of 4 years and 237 days.

Form No. 2.

NEW ZEALAND EXPEDITIONARY FORCE.

ATTESTATION OF

No. Name: Mc Bride Joseph Bell Regiment or Unit:

Questions to be put to the recruit before enlistment.

1. What is your name? ... 1. McBRIDE Joseph Bell
2. Where were you born? ... 2. Charlton
3. Are you a British subject? ... 3. Yes
4. What is the date of your birth? ... 4. 25th October 1892
5. What is your trade or calling? ... 5. Student
6. Are you an indentured apprentice? If so, where, and to whom? 6. No
7. What was the address at which you last resided? ... 7. 389 Castle Str. Dunedin
8. Have you passed the Fourth Educational Standard or its equivalent? 8. Yes
9. What is the name and address of your present or last employer? 9. None
10. Are you married? 10. No.
11. Have you ever been sentenced to imprisonment by the Civil power? If so, when and where? 11. No
12. Do you now belong to any military or naval force? If so, to what corps? 12. Yes. A. Company 4th Reg. N.Z.R
13. Have you ever served in any military or naval force? If so, state which and cause of discharge. 13. No.
14. Have you truly stated the whole (if any) of your previous service? 14. Yes
15. Have you been registered for compulsory military training under the Defence Act, 1909? If so, where? 15. Yes; Gore transferred Dunedin
16. Have you ever been rejected as unfit for the military or naval forces of the Crown? If so, on what grounds? 16. No
17. Are you willing to be vaccinated or revaccinated? 17. Yes.
18. Are you willing to serve in the Expeditionary Force in or beyond the Dominion of New Zealand under the following conditions, provided your services should so long be required: For the term of the present European war and for such further period as is necessary to bring the Expeditionary Force back to New Zealand and to disband it? 18. Yes

NOTE.—Your discharge will not be granted before your return to New Zealand unless permission for discharge elsewhere be obtained from the G.O.C. the New Zealand Expeditionary Force.

I, Joseph Bell McBride, do solemnly declare that the above answers made by me to the above questions are true, and that I am willing to fulfil the engagement made.

Signature of Recruit: Joseph B. McBride

Signature of Witness: Eugene J O'Neill

Oath to be taken by recruit on attestation.

I, Joseph Bell McBride, do sincerely promise and swear that I will be faithful and bear true allegiance to our Sovereign Lord the King, his Heirs and Successors, and that I will faithfully serve in the New Zealand Military Forces, according to my liability under the Defence Act, and that I will observe and obey all orders of His Majesty, his Heirs and Successors, and of the Generals and Officers set over me, until I shall be lawfully discharged. So help me, God!

Certificate of Magistrate or Attesting Officer.

The above questions were read to the above-named recruit in my presence. I have taken care that he understands each question, and that his answer to each question has been duly entered as replied to, and the said recruit has made and signed the declaration and taken the oath before me, at ____, N.Z., on this 6th day of Aug, 1914

Signature of Attesting Officer: Eugene J O'Neill

If any alteration is required on this page of the Attestation, the Attesting Officer should be requested to make it and initial the alteration.

Eugene O'Neill witnessed
Joseph McBride's enlistment
to the New Zealand Expeditionary Force,
August 1914.

2

Description of Mc Bride, Joseph Bell **on Enlistment.**

Apparent age: 21 years 9 months.
(To be determined according to the instructions given in the Regulations for Army Medical Service).

Height: 5 feet 5½ inches.
Weight: 9. 12 lb.
Chest-measurement: Minimum, 34 inches. Maximum, 36½ inches.
Complexion: fair
Colour of eyes: Hazel
Colour of hair: fair
Religious profession: Presbyterian

Distinctive marks, and marks indicating congenital peculiarities or previous disease.

Medical Examination.

Sight: Right eye, 6/6
Left eye, 6/6
Hearing: Right ear, good
Left ear, good
Colour-vision: Good
Are his limbs well formed? Yes.
Are the movements of all his joints full and perfect? Yes.
Is his chest well formed? Yes
Is his heart normal? Yes
Are his lungs normal? Yes.
What is the condition of the teeth? [illegible]

Is he free from hernia? Yes
Is he free from varicocele? Yes
Is he free from varicose veins? Yes
Is he free from hæmorrhoids? Yes.
Is he free from inveterate or contagious skin-disease? Yes.
Is there a distinct mark of vaccination? Yes.
Is he in good bodily and mental health and free from any physical defect likely to interfere with the efficient performance of his duties? Yes.
Are there any slight defects, but not sufficient to cause rejection?

Remarks.

[illegible]

Certificate of Medical Examination.

I have examined the above-named, and find he does not present any of the causes of rejection specified in the Regulations for Army Medical Services.

I consider him fit for service in the New Zealand Expeditionary Force.

18 Aug, 1914 [illegible], Medical Officer.

21 years and 9 months old. Fair
complexion, hazel eyes, fair hair.
Presbyterian religion.

No. 4 N.Z. FIELD AMBULANCE
Army Form B. 103.

Casualty Form—Active Service.

Regiment or Corps Auckland Infy. H.Q. N.Z.M.C. Attached .... Battn. ....

Regimental No. 12/1127 Rank Private Name McBride, Joseph Bell

Enlisted (a) 18/8/14 Terms of Service (a) Duration of War Service reckons from (a) 18/8/14

Date of promotion to present rank ____ Date of appointment to lance rank ____ Numerical position on roll of N.C.Os. ____

Extended ____ Re-engaged ____ Qualification (b) Medical Duties

Report: Date	Report: From whom received	Record of promotions, reductions, transfers, casualties, etc., during active service, as reported on Army Form B. 213, Army Form A. 36, or in other official documents. The authority to be quoted in each case.	Place	Date	Remarks taken from Army Form B. 213, Army Form A. 36, or other official documents.
		Embarked for Dardanelles	Alexandria	12/4/15	Embarkation Roll
12-12-15	H.S. Oxfordshire	admitted to H.S. Oxfordshire	Dardanelles	12/12/15	Jaundice Roll 3197

Embarked for Dardenelles Alexandria 12th Apr 1914

Admitted to H.S Oxfordshire, Dardenelles 12th Dec, 1915.

Admitted to NZ Gen Hospital, Cairo, Egypt, 15th Dec 1915.

Discharged to Base Depot, Ghezirah, Egypt 31st Dec 1915.

Rejoined unit. Ismailia, Egypt, 18th Jan 1916.

Attached to ___ Camp, Ismailia, Egypt, 10th Feb 1916.

Attached for duty, Ismailia, Egypt, 2nd Mar, 1916.

Rejoined unit, Ismailia, Egypt, 7th Mar, 1916

Attached for 1st Batt, Ismailia, Egypt, 25th Mar, 1916.

Embarked for France, Almeria, France, 6th Apr 1916.

Joined No1. IF Amb, France, 2nd Aug 1916.

Promoted to Corporal, 13th Oct 1915.

2nd base NZFA for duty, France, 12th Nov, 1916.

Joined No1. IF Amb, France, 11th Feb, 1917.

20th Mar, 1917.

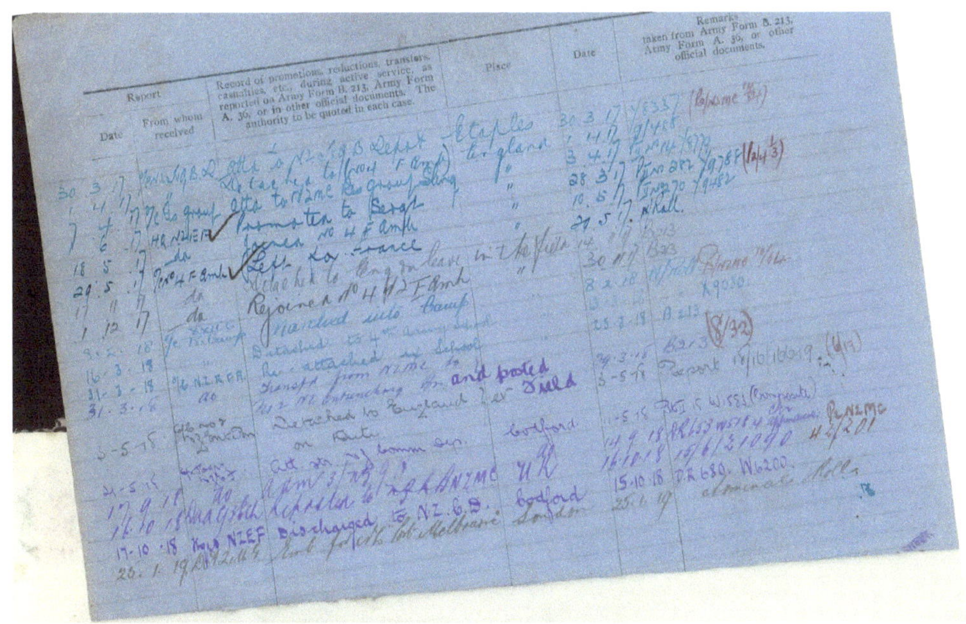

Report		Record of promotions, reductions, transfers, casualties, etc., during active service, as reported on Army Form B. 213, Army Form A. 36, or in other official documents. The authority to be quoted in each case.	Place	Date	Remarks taken from Army Form B. 213, Army Form A. 36, or other official documents.
Date	From whom received				

Attached to NZ A B Depot, Etaples, 30th Mar, 1917

Detached to F. Amb, England, 1st Apr 1917.

Attached to NZ __, England, 3rd Apr, 1917.

Promoted to Sergeant, England, 28th Mar 1917.

Joined No. 4 F Amb, England, 10th May 1917.

Left for France, England 20th May 1917.

Attached to England on leave in the field, 14th Nov 1917.

Rejoined No. 4 NZ F Amb in the field, 30th Nov, 1917.

___ into camp, in the field, 8th Feb 1918.

Detached to 4th Army School in the field, 13th Mar 1918.

Reattached in School in the field, 23rd Mar 1918.

Transfer from NZMC to NZ Entrenching Brigade and posted in field, 24th Mar 1918.

Detached to England on duty, 3rd May, 1918.

___ NZ Comm Dep, Codford, England, 11th May 1918.

Adm ___ 14th Sep 1918.

Reposted to NZMC, U.K, 16th Oct 1918.

Discharged to NZ_D, Codford, England, 15th Oct, 1918.

Embarked for Melbourne. 25th Jan, 1919

NEW ZEALAND EXPEDITIONARY FORCE.

N.Z. Medical Corps

Rank Cpl. (Sgt.) Name McBride Joseph Bell Unit [illegible] No. 12/1124

Enltd. 18/8/14 M. or S. S. D. of Birth 25/10/92 Occupn. Student Ht. 5' 5½" Wt. 9st 12 lbs.

Hair Fair Eyes Hazel Complexn. Fair Relgn. Presby Inocln.

N.K. Father, L. McBride, Charlton, Via Gore N.Z.

PROMOTIONS, CASUALTIES, MOVEMENTS, etc.	DATE OF CASUALTY.	AUTHORITY AND DATE OF SAME.	INITIALS.
Joined No. 1 Fld. Amb.	11.2.14	1 F. Amb. [illegible]	[illegible]
Detached to 1st Bde N.Z.F.A. for duty	20.3.17	[illegible]	[illegible]
Attached to N.Z.I. & G.B.D.	30.3.17	[illegible]	[illegible]
Marched in from France & attached to [illegible]	3.4.17	[illegible]	[illegible]
Taken on [illegible] & posted to [illegible] Amb Blackpool	10.5.17	[illegible]	[illegible]
To be Sergeant	28.3.17	[illegible]	[illegible]
		[illegible]	[illegible]
[illegible] Amb France	3.2.18	[illegible]	[illegible]
AT CHEDDIELCOTTS REINFT CAMP	[illegible]	[illegible]	[illegible]
[illegible] Bedford [illegible]	[illegible]	[illegible]	[illegible]
Detached to Eng. on Duty	3.5.18	[illegible]	[illegible]
JOINED [illegible]		[illegible]	[illegible]
[illegible]	14.9.18	[illegible]	[illegible]
To C. Blford [illegible]	15.10.18	[illegible]	[illegible]

Sergt. McBride Joseph Bell 12/1124

N.Z. Medical Corps

PROMOTIONS, CASUALTIES, MOVEMENTS, etc.	DATE OF CASUALTY.	AUTHORITY AND DATE OF SAME.	INITIALS.
Re-posted to N.Z. Med Corps	16.10.18	[illegible]	[illegible]

EMB FOR NZ FORT MELBOURNE

25.1.19

16.10.14 7.3.19.

[B.R. Form No. 207A.

No. 41074 19.3.19

NEW ZEALAND EXPEDITIONARY FORCE.

CERTIFICATE OF DISCHARGE.

No. 10/1127 Rank: Sergeant Unit: N Z Entrenching Batt.

Name: Joseph Bell McBride

is discharged on the termination of his period of engagement.

Service abroad: 4 years 143 days.

DESCRIPTION OF SOLDIER ON ENLISTMENT.

Age: 21 4/12 Years Height: 5 feet 5 1/2 inches

Complexion: Fair Eyes: Hazel

Hair: Fair. Trade or occupation: Student

PARCHMENT DISCHARGE POSTED. Date 21.3.19

Signature:

Wellington, 11 April, 1919. For Major-General, Commanding New Zealand Military Forces.

N.B.—(1.) This certificate is issued without alteration or erasure of any kind. (2.) Any person finding this certificate is requested to forward it to Headquarters, Military Forces, Wellington, N.Z. (3.) Should this certificate be lost or mislaid no duplicate of it can be obtained.

[B.R.—No. 89.

CONFIDENTIAL.

PROCEEDINGS OF A PROVISIONAL MEDICAL BOARD

Assembled on board the Troopship "____," at the Port of ____, by order of Commandant, New Zealand Military Forces, for the purpose of examining and recommending treatment for—

No. ____ Rank: ____ Name: ____

Unit: ____

____, President.

____ Members.

1. The Board, having assembled, receive from the medical officer in charge of the above soldier his report on the case, together with previous medical papers, examine and attach same to the proceedings.

2. The Board finds that the soldier is suffering from the following disability:

3. The Board finds that the soldier is still requiring treatment, and recommends he receive treatment—

(a.) As an in-patient of hospital, convalescent home, or sanatorium at

(b.) As an out-patient of hospital at ____ whilst residing at ____

(c.) Under private arrangements, at his own request, which is in writing attached, whilst residing at ____

4. The Board finds the soldier is no longer requiring treatment, and recommends

(Signatures) ____, President. ____ Members.

Date: ____

Approved.

Wellington, For Surgeon-General, Director-General Medical Services.

Date: ____

N.Z./M.6

ABRIDGED MEDICAL BOARD ON NON COMMISSIONED OFFICERS AND MEN N.Z.E.F.

N.Z. Command Depot.
Codford.

12/1127

Station Codford.
Date 16 JAN 1919

1. Unit N.Z.M.C.
2. Regimental No. 12/1127
3. Rank Sgt.
4. Name McBride J. B.
5. Age last birthday 26
6. Enlisted (on 17 August 1914 (at Dunedin
7. Former trade or occupation Student
8. Disability

9. Place and date of origin of disability:-

10. Essential facts in the history of the disability:-

11. Causation of the disability:-

12. Present condition of the patient:-

13. Recommendation of the Medical Officer:- B_2 (Sig.)

OPINION OF THE MEDICAL BOARD.

14. (a) State whether disability result of (1) active service, (2) climate, or (3) ordinary military service.
(b) If due to one of these causes, to what specific conditions do the Board attribute it? By infection on A.S.
(c) Is the disability constitutional or hereditary?

15. Note if aggravated by intemperance, misconduct, or the conditions mentioned in Section 14 (a). see 14.

16. Is the disability permanent? If not, state probable minimum duration:- No 2 months.

17. State the degree of disablement at which, in the Board's opinion, he should be assessed for pension purposes at present. By less than 20%.
Express in percentages:- 100, 80, 70, 60, 50, 40, 30, 20, less than 20, nil

18. Recommendation of the Board:- B 2 (two).

Signatures:- Major, N.Z.M.C. President, S.M.B.

N.Z. Command Depot.
Codford.

Station
Date

N.Z. Command Depot.
Codford.

Station
Date

APPROVED.

Administrative Medical Officer.

N.Z./M.6

ABRIDGED MEDICAL BOARD ON NON COMMISSIONED OFFICERS AND MEN N.Z.E.F.

N.Z. Command Depot.
Codford.

12/1127

Station Codford.
Date 16 JAN 1919

1. Unit N.Z.M.C.
2. Regimental No. 12/1127
3. Rank Sgt.
4. Name McBride J. B.
5. Age last birthday 26
6. Enlisted (on 17 August 1914 (at Dunedin
7. Former trade or occupation Student
8. Disability

9. Place and date of origin of disability:-

10. Essential facts in the history of the disability:-

11. Causation of the disability:-

12. Present condition of the patient:-

13. Recommendation of the Medical Officer:- B_2 (Sig.)

OPINION OF THE MEDICAL BOARD.

14. (a) State whether disability result of (1) active service, (2) climate, or (3) ordinary military service.
(b) If due to one of these causes, to what specific conditions do the Board attribute it? By infection on A.S.
(c) Is the disability constitutional or hereditary?

15. Note if aggravated by intemperance, misconduct, or the conditions mentioned in Section 14 (a). see 14.

16. Is the disability permanent? If not, state probable minimum duration:- No 2 months.

17. State the degree of disablement at which, in the Board's opinion, he should be assessed for pension purposes at present. By less than 20%.
Express in percentages:- 100, 80, 70, 60, 50, 40, 30, 20, less than 20, nil

18. Recommendation of the Board:- B 2 (two).

Signatures:- Major, N.Z.M.C. President, S.M.B.

N.Z. Command Depot.
Codford.

Station
Date

N.Z. Command Depot.
Codford.

Station
Date

APPROVED.

Administrative Medical Officer.

Army Form B. 178

To be used (a) for recruits enlisting direct into the Regular Army, and (b) for men of the Territorial Force when they are admitted to Hospital. Army Form B. 178A to be used for Special Reserve recruits and Special Reservists enlisting into the Regular Army.

MEDICAL HISTORY OF

Surname McBride *Christian Name* J. (Sgt)

TABLE I.—General Table.

Birthplace { Parish .... County ....

Examined { on .... day of .... 191 at ....

Declared Age .... years .... days.

Trade or Occupation ....

Height .... feet .... inches

Weight .... lbs.

Chest Measurement { Girth when fully Expanded .... inches; Range of Expansion .... inches

Physical Development ....

Vaccination Marks { Arm — RIGHT — LEFT; Number

When Vaccinated ....

Vision { R.E.—V= .... L.E.—V= ....

(a) Marks indicating congenital peculiarities or previous disease—

(b) Slight defects but not sufficient to cause rejection—

Approved by ....

Rank .... *Medical Officer.*

Enlisted { at .... on .... day of 191

	Corps	Regtl. No.
Joined on enlistment		
Transferred to	[illegible]	12/[illegible]

Became non-effective by ....

on .... day of 191

(Signature) ....

(Rank) ....

TABLE III.—Boards; Courts of Enquiry, Vaccination, Inoculations, etc.; Examinations for Field or Foreign Service, Extension, Re-engagement, or Prolongation of Service; Issue of Surgical Appliances; Particulars of Dental Treatment, etc.

Date	Brief Details and Signature
	B 2 (two)
	Fred H Bowerbank, N.Z.M.C., President, M.B.

TABLE IV.—Service Table.

Station or Troopship	Date of arrival or embarkation	Date of departure or disembarkation

[11,823] W2830/M2217 1,800,000 6/17 W. P. & Co. (1348)

TABLE II.—Only for admissions to Hospital or to the Sick List in case of Warrant Officers treated in quarters.

Name of Hospital	Admitted to Hospital Day	Month	Year	Discharged from Hospital Day	Month	Year	Disease	Number of days in Hospital	Remarks bearing on the cause, nature, or treatment of the case, likely to be of interest or of future use. In cases of syphilis, admissions and re-admissions to hospital will be shown. The subsequent progress, including particulars of treatment out of hospital, transfers, &c., will be given in the special syphilis case sheet.	Signature of Medical Officer
No 3 NZGH	14	9	18	14	10	18	Appendicitis	30	Two months attacks of subacute appendicitis. 20/9/18 Appendicectomy. Thickened appendix … 14/10/18 Discharge Depot 14 days …	[illegible] Capt.

NEW ZEALAND EXPEDITIONARY FORCE. 13 19 Form No. 3.

MILITARY HISTORY SHEET.

No. Name: McBride Joseph Bell

	Country.	From.	To.	Years.	Days.	Initials of Officer making entry.
1. Service record.						

2. Certificates.

3. Passed classes of instruction. (This includes any authorized class of instruction.) — St John Ryan

4. Active service

5. Wounded

6. Effects of wounds

7. Special instances of gallant or meritorious conduct.

	Name of Medal.	Class.	Date of Grant.
8. Medals and decorations.			

9. Injuries in or by the Service.

10. Name and address of next-of-kin. — Mr R. McBride, Charlton, nr Gore

11. Particulars as to Marriage.	(a) Christian and Surname of Woman to whom married, and whether Spinster or Widow	(b) Place and Date of Marriage.	(c) Name of Officiating Minister or Registrar.

12. Particulars as to Children.	Christian Names.	Date and Place of Birth.	Where registered.

NOTE.—These entries are to be made from time to time as they occur, and initialled by the officer making the entry.

Intended place of residence on discharge :

STATEMENT OF THE SERVICES OF No. NAME: McBride Joseph Bell

Regiment or Corps.	Promotions, Reductions, Casualties, etc.	Rank.	Dates.	Signature of Officer certifying Correctness of Entries.

J. Anderson, Printer, Auckland.—9298

NEW ZEALAND EXPEDITIONARY FORCE. [Form No. 3.

MILITARY HISTORY SHEET.

No. 12/1127 Name: McBride Joseph Bell

	Country.	From	To	Years.	Days.	Initials of Officer making Entry.
1. Service Record	New Zealand	18.8.14	12.10.14	.	56	LHR
	At Sea 10.12	13.10.14	3.12.14	.	52	LHR
	Egypt	4.12.14				

2. Certificates ...

3. Passed classes of instruction† (†This includes any authorised class of instruction.)

4. Active service ...

5. Wounded ...

6. Effects of wounds ...

7. Special instances of gallant or meritorious conduct ...

8. Medals and decorations ...

Name of Medal.	Clasps.	Date of Grant.

9. Injuries in or by the Service...

10. Name and address of next-of-kin ... (father) L. McBride Charlton Via Gore New Zealand

11. Particulars as to Marriage. (a.) Christian and Surname of Woman to whom married, and whether Spinster or Widow. (b.) Place and Date of Marriage. (c.) Name of Officiating Minister or Registrar.

(a)	(b)	(c)

Particulars as to Children.

Christian Names.	Date and Place of Birth.	Where registered.

Note.—These entries are to be made from time to time as they occur, and initialled by the officer making the entry.

Place of residence on discharge ...

STATEMENT OF THE SERVICES OF No. 12/1127 NAME: McBride Joseph Bell

Regiment or Corps.	Promotions, Reductions, Casualties, etc.	Rank.	Dates.	Signature of Officer certifying Correctness of Entries.
N.Z. M.C. attached Aust. Infantry Battn.	Attested	Pte.	18.8.14	L.H. Rad. Sergt.
	[illegible] Somalia from N.Z. General Base Depot		18/[illegible]/14	[illegible]
	Attd. to N.Z. Fld. Amb. [illegible] Somalia for [illegible]		10/2/1[illegible]	[illegible]
N.Z.F. Artillery 2nd Bde	Detached for duty	.	2.3.16	R. McKenzie
1st Bn A.I.R.	Attached	.	23.3.16	R.M.
No1 F. Amb.	Joined No1 F. Amb. (No1 F. Amb. P.II O.15)	.	2.8.16	[illegible]
	Promoted (No1 [illegible])	Cpl	13.10.16	B.E. Champion
	Detached to 1st Bde. N.Z.F.A. for duty (No1 Fld. Amb. P.II [illegible] 25/11/16)	.	12.11.16	H. Owens

[Form No. 4.

NEW ZEALAND EXPEDITIONARY FORCE.

MEDICAL HISTORY

OF

Surname: McBride   Christian Name: Joseph Bell

Examined: On 15th day of Aug 1914
At Auckland

Birthplace: Town Charlton
Country New Zealand

Declared age: 21 year 9 months

Trade or occupation: Student

Height: 5 ft. 5½ in.

Weight: 13[illegible] lb.

Chest measurement: Minimum 36 in.
Maximum expansion 36½ in.

Physical development:

Small-pox marks:

Vaccination marks: Right. Left.
Arm
Number

When vaccinated:

Marks indicating congenital peculiarities or previous disease:

Approved by

Medical Officer

Examined for re-engagement:

day of 191

*Considered:

Medical Officer

*If unfit, state disability.

Re-vaccinated on day of 191

Arm: Number:

Result:

Medical Officer

Enlisted on 15th day of Aug. 1914. at Dunedin

	Corps.	Regimental No.	Date.
Joined on enlistment	N. Z. M. C. attached Auck Infy Battn	12/1127	15 8 14
Transferred to			

PROPOSED FOR DISCHARGE BY A MEDICAL BOARD.

Station.	Date.	Disease.	Result.

This sheet to be disposed of in accordance with instructions in the Regulations for Army Medical Services on the man becoming non-effective, the date and cause being stated at the foot of next page.

Anderson, Printer, Auckland

Name: McBride   Christian Name: Joseph Bell

Station or Troopship.	Date of Arrival at the Station or at Embarkation	Dates of Admission into Hospital			Dates of Discharge from Hospital			Disease.	Number of Days in Hospital	Remarks on Nature of Disease; How induced, if mild or severe, if completely recovered from, whether any particular treatment was adopted. In venereal disease state nature of primary disease and whether mercury has been given. If an accident state whether it occurred on duty and whether a court of inquiry was held.	Signature of Medical Officer.
		Day	Mon.	Year	Day	Mon.	Year				

www.ingramcontent.com/pod-product-compliance
Lightning Source LLC
Chambersburg PA
CBHW042012090426
42811CB00015B/1623
* 9 7 8 0 4 7 3 4 3 9 1 2 5 *